BIBLICAL

TYPOLOGY

Based on the Original Studies by

BARRY CHANT

BIBLICAL TYPOLOGY

Based on the Original Studies of

BARRY CHANT

Copyright © 2012 Ken Chant

ISBN:978-1-61529-091-8

Vision Publishing
1672 Main St. E 109
Ramona, CA 92065
1-800-9-VISION
www.booksbyvision.com

A NOTE ON GENDER

It is unfortunate that the English language does not contain an adequate generic pronoun (especially in the singular number) that includes without bias both male and female. So *"he, him, his, man, mankind,"* with their plurals, must do the work for both sexes. Accordingly, wherever it is appropriate to do so in the following pages, please include the feminine gender in the masculine, and vice versa.

FOOTNOTES

A work once fully referenced will thereafter be noted either by "ibid" or "op. cit."

TABLE OF CONTENTS

Plan of the tabernacle, and other pictures

Description - problems - two-fold significance: historical and typical - fanciful theories.

The tabernacle itself - names, construction, components - the two curtains - the frame - interpretation - erection of the structure - the veil and screen

Outer court: the altar, the laver - the holy place: the table of show-bread, the lampstand, the altar of incense - the holy of holies: the ark, the cherubim.

The garments of the high priest - the Urim and Thummim - the families responsible to care for the tabernacle - its later history.

The right/wrong way to handle typology - the central meaning of the tabernacle - a basic rule of interpretation - some possible interpretations - more detailed symbolism of the cloud, the structure, the colours and materials, the area, the furnishings, the high priest's garments, etc.

The three great feasts - how they should be interpreted - the nature of the feasts - their significance - when they were held - the purpose of the sacrificial system - various offerings and their significance - when they were offered.

The Passover - description and history - why and how this feast was held - the sacrifices - Israel's observance of Passover - significance of the feast - typology of the feast - current Jewish practice.

Pentecost - background and history - why the feast was held - described by Josephus - the significance of the feast to Christians.

Tabernacles - background - what was this feast? - why and how this feast was observed - the festival of booths - the use of trumpets in the OT - further details on the three major parts of this feast.

The significance of the Feast of Tabernacles for Christians - the Hebrew year - relationship of the feasts - a false typology examined - principles of a true typology - chart of the feasts.

ABBREVIATIONS

Abbreviations commonly used for the books of the Bible are

Genesis	Ge	Habakkuk	Hb
Exodus	Ex	Zephaniah	Zp
Leviticus	Le	Haggai	Hg
Numbers	Nu	Zechariah	Zc
Deuteronomy	De	Malachi	Mal
Joshua	Js		
Judges	Jg		
Ruth	Ru	Matthew	Mt
1 Samuel	1 Sa	Mark	Mk
2 Samuel	2 Sa	Luke	Lu
1 Kings	1 Kg	John	Jn
2 Kings	2 Kg	Acts	Ac
1 Chronicles	1 Ch	Romans	Ro
2 Chronicles	2 Ch	1 Corinthians	1 Co
Ezra	Ezr	2 Corinthians	2 Co
Nehemiah	Ne	Galatians	Ga
Esther	Es	Ephesians	Ep
Job	Jb	Philippians	Ph
Psalm	Ps	Colossians	Cl
Proverbs	Pr	1 Thessalonians	1 Th
Ecclesiastes	Ec	2 Thessalonians	2 Th
Song of Songs	Ca *	1 Timothy	1 Ti
Isaiah	Is	2 Timothy	2 Ti
Jeremiah	Je	Titus	Tit
Lamentations	La	Philemon	Phm
Ezekiel	Ez	Hebrews	He
Daniel	Da	James	Ja
Hosea	Ho	1 Peter	1 Pe
Joel	Jl	2 Peter	2 Pe
Amos	Am	1 John	1 Jn
Obadiah	Ob	2 John	2 Jn
Jonah	Jo	3 John	3 Jn
Micah	Mi	Jude	Ju
Nahum	Na	Revelation	Re

Ca is an abbreviation of *Canticles*, a derivative of the Latin name of the *Song of Solomon*, which is sometimes also called the *Song of Songs*.

Acknowledgments: the illustrations in this book were drawn and kindly donated by the artist Gill Waddle, of Tasmania. Scripture translations are copyright by *VCC*, unless otherwise noted.

THE TABERNACLE
Drawn to scale: 1 cm = 5cubits (furniture not to scale)

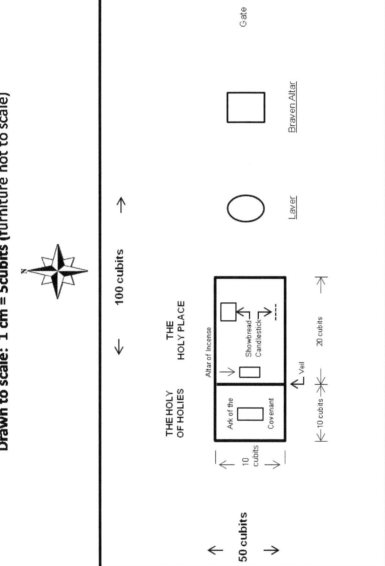

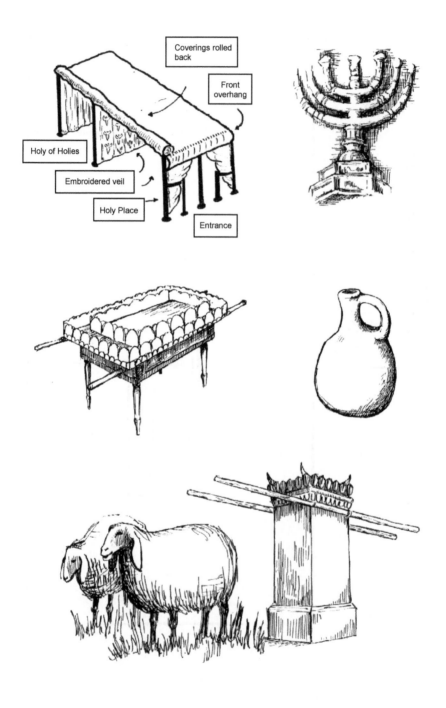

Coverings rolled back

Front overhang

Holy of Holies

Embroidered veil

Holy Place

Entrance

CHAPTER ONE

THE TABERNACLE

Imagine a fifteen-by-forty-five-foot house, constructed of three tons of gold, five tons of silver, four tons of brass, and an assortment of jewels, fine wood, and fancy tapestries.

This was the tabernacle, the portable house of worship built by a horde of escaped slaves. In the providence of God, the amazing project was financed by the farewell gifts to the children of Israel by their erstwhile captors, the Egyptians. . . The unique structure and value of the tabernacle command our attention. Never before nor since has there been such a costly prefab structure. . . [1]

You will find a drawing of this tabernacle on the previous pages, and you should try to visualise it as the focal point of Israel's worship for at least 300 years - that is, from the time of Moses to the erection of Solomon's temple. [2] During those three centuries the liturgies and sacrifices prescribed for the service of the tabernacle were sometimes scrupulously observed, and sometimes almost entirely ignored. Nonetheless, it seems that the tabernacle never lacked an attendant priest, and it remained in more or less continual use right up until the day it was finally dismantled and transferred with all of its equipment to Solomon's temple. It

---

[1] C. Sumner Wemp, Teaching From the Tabernacle; Moody Press, Chicago, 1976; pg. 13.
[2] Allowing approximately 1280 BC as the date of the Exodus, and approximately 950 BC as the date of the Temple.

is probable that the Ark of the Covenant was the only piece of the original furniture used in the temple. Solomon rebuilt all of the other furniture, probably on a larger scale, and then stored the original tabernacle, its vessels and its furnishings, in the temple as sacred relics.

PROBLEMS

There are many problems associated with any attempt to interpret the data given in scripture about the tabernacle. Some parts of the structure are described in extraordinary detail, while the descriptions of other parts are remarkably vague. Confusion exists as to whether there were <u>two</u> structures called *"the tent of meeting"* and *"the tabernacle"*, or whether both names referred to the same sanctuary. There is debate about the history of the tabernacle, about many of the measurements that are given, about the design and appearance of the main structure and of each item of furniture, about the typical significance of the various objects and ceremonies, and so on.

This study will not enter into these disputes. If you desire more information on the historicity of the tabernacle, its place in the national life of Israel, the difficulties associated with its design and function, its similarity to other portable sanctuaries that were used in Bible lands prior to the time of Moses, the problems which exist in the scripture datum itself, then you should turn to any major conservative commentary on Exodus, or to a comprehensive Bible Encyclopaedia.

The stance adopted in these notes is

- The tabernacle was a truly historical structure.

- The biblical records are accurate and reliable in all that they assert concerning the tabernacle.

- That difficulties in interpreting the text result from insufficient information, not from textual errors.

- That an understanding of the various types should be sought which is cautious and in complete harmony with the teaching of the NT. However, no infallibility is claimed for the explanations and applications offered in the following pages. Generally I have preferred a fairly standard interpretation, and I have sought to maintain a uniform presentation. Extreme positions have been avoided (although I know that there are some who think that any position is extreme which attempts to give even a modestly detailed application of the tabernacle to present Christian experience.) There are many different ways to approach biblical typology, and what is presented here does not by any means exhaust the available options.

WHY BOTHER?

At this point someone may ask, "Why bother with the subject at all?" As one anonymous enquirer put it: "Why should we study an ancient structure used by people long since deceased, to perform religious rites no longer observed?"

The answer is given to us by the apostles -

> *Now these things (the experiences of ancient Israel) . . . were written down for our instruction, upon whom the end of the ages has come (1 Co 10:11) . . . (which) the Holy Spirit indicates . . . is symbolic for this present age (He 9:1-9).*

So the tabernacle has a two-fold significance -

HISTORICAL

The tabernacle with its priests and their ministry was foundational to the religious life of Israel. The basic concept was that which underlays the theocracy itself: the Lord dwelling in visible glory in his sanctuary among his people (Ex 25:8) . . . (It has value) because of its embodiment of important religious and spiritual concepts. It reveals:

- the necessary conditions upon which Israel could maintain fellowship in covenant relationship with the Lord;

- the dominant truth of the presence of God in the midst of his people (29:25), a dwelling that must conform in every detail with his divine character, that is, his unity and holiness. One God requires one sanctuary; the holy God demands a holy people (Le 19:2).

- the perfection and harmony of the Lord's character seen in the aesthetics of the tabernacle's architecture, the gradations in metals and materials, the degrees of sanctity exhibited in the court, the holy place, and the holiest, and the measurements of the tabernacle . . . [3]

TYPICAL

The NT repeatedly cites different features (of the tabernacle, and uses them) to teach deep spiritual truth . . . The Mount of Transfiguration experience (Mt 17:4; etc.) harks back to the tabernacle of Moses. John in his prologue (1:14) makes much of the Incarnation of the Lord Jesus Christ as the tabernacling among men. The testimony of Stephen (Ac 7:44) is unmistakable. Paul directly equates the cross of Calvary as God's mercy seat, or propitiatory, in finalising the

[3] Pictorial Encyclopedia of the Bible, Vol. 5, pg. 583; Merrill C. Tenney, gen. ed. Zondervan Publishing House, Michigan, 1975.

redemption of sinful man (Ro 3:25). In speaking of regeneration he had in mind the laver in Tit 3:5. The proper interpretation of Cl 1:19 and 2:9 will relate them to the dwelling presence of God in the tabernacle of old. The epistle to the Hebrews is inexplicable without the teaching of the worship of Israel and their priesthood residing in the tabernacle. Passages such as Re 8:3, 4; 13:6; 15:5; 21:3 are too clear to need comment. [4]

These things, and many others, are explored in the pages that follow.

FANCIFUL THEORIES

Over the centuries there have been some bizarre theories linked with the tabernacle -

> When Moses distinguished the tabernacle into three parts, and allowed two of them to the priests, as a place accessible and common, he denoted the land and the sea, these being of general access to all; but he set `part the third division for God, because heaven is inaccessible to men. And when he ordered twelve loaves to be set on the table, he denoted the year, as distinguished into so many months. By branching out the candlestick into seventy parts, he secretly intimated the "Decani", or seventy divisions of the planets; and as to the seven lamps upon the candlesticks, they referred to the course of the planets, of which that is the number. The veils, too, which were composed of four things, they declared the four elements; for the fine linen was proper to signify the earth, because the flax grows out of the earth; the purple signified the sea, because

---

[4] Ibid pg. 582.

that colour is dyed by the blood of a sea shell-fish; the blue is to signify the air; and the scarlet will naturally be an indication of fire. . . [5]

Josephus continues in a similar way to give a symbolic meaning to other parts of the tabernacle. His theories bear scant resemblance to modern interpretations of the typology of the tabernacle, but they probably have as much reason behind them! For while we find it strange that Josephus saw in the tabernacle a picture of the entire universe, his ideas are no more fanciful than many that the church has spawned over the centuries. Some teachers have ascribed a profound meaning almost to every thread and splinter of the structure, and to every detail of its furnishings and ceremonies; while others have reacted to the point of denying that the edifice has any relevance to the modern church. These notes will hopefully find a moderate, yet still scriptural position.

THE TABERNACLE

The principal descriptions of the tabernacle are found in Exodus ch. 25-40 and Numbers ch. 3, 4, 7, and 8. You should carefully read at least the Exodus chapters, and at the same time refer to the diagram on pages 5 & 6, which represents a fair consensus on the probable appearance of the structure. [6] C. W. Slemming describes it this way - [7]

---

[5] Josephus, Antiquities, Book 3, Ch. 7, Sec. 7.

[6] Josephus gives a fine and detailed description in his Antiquities (Book 3, Ch. 6), which I nearly included here, but was hindered by its length.

[7] Made According To Pattern, pg. 16-17; Christian Literature Crusade, Fort Washington, Pennsylvania, 1974 reprint. This is one of a series of three books by Charles Slemming; the other two are: "These Are The Garments," a study on the robes of the High Priest; and, "Thus Shalt Thou Serve," a study on the offerings and feasts. Slemming does not discuss any of the historical and critical issues that surround the

(The tabernacle) was made *"according to the pattern of things in the heavenlies,"* which things were revealed to Moses while in the mount. It was, so it would appear, the pattern that was later shown to John while he was on the Isle of Patmos, for we find in the Revelation: an altar of sacrifice (Re 6:9); a sea of glass (4:6); seven golden candlesticks (1:12); the golden altar (8:3); hidden manna (2:17); and the ark of his testament (11:19). Repeatedly in both Exodus and Hebrews the Lord said: *"See that you make it according to the pattern."* God was very particular in planning it, no doubt Moses was in the building of it, and ought not we to be in the understanding of it?

If the amount of space devoted to a subject in scripture is a criterion of its importance, then the tabernacle must rank highly. In an unpublished set of lecture notes, Hal Oxley gives the following statistics

> Exodus .... 15 chapters
> Leviticus .... 18 chapters
> Numbers .... 13 chapters
> Deuteronomy .... 2 chapters
> Hebrews .... 3 chapters

The total shows that no less than *51 chapters* of scripture deal with the tabernacle.

In addition to these extensive references to the tabernacle itself, there are also many references to the temple, which

---

tabernacle, but his three books are excellent and detailed devotional studies.

was based on the tabernacle design (e.g. 1 Kg. 5 ff; Ez 40 ff; etc.)

THE NAMES OF THE TABERNACLE

Several Hebrew names are used in the Bible for the tabernacle. They are sometimes used interchangeably, which is a source of confusion, especially when some English versions translate the various Hebrew words in different ways. The RSV translates them consistently.

Here is a list of the terms used -

TABERNACLE

(Hebrew, "*mishkan*" = dwelling)

This word is normally used only in poetry (Ps 76: 2; Ca 1:8). In Exodus it is used in two ways -

- it is the name of the inner covering of the tabernacle, a fine twined linen curtain, richly embroidered. This covering is always called the "*mishkan*", perhaps because it formed the actual ceiling and walls of the tabernacle - thus it turned the building from an empty frame into a true *"dwelling"* (Ex 26:1; 36:8).

- it is used to designate the wooden frame-work (Ex 36:20; 40:18); and also the whole structure (Ex 40: 33, 34; Nu 1:51; etc.)

TENT

(Hebrew "*ohel*" = tent)

This is the common word for a tent (Ge 9:21; etc.) In Exodus "*ohel*" refers primarily to the goats' hair covering that was placed immediately on top of the linen "*mishkan*" (Ex 26:7; 36:14); but with qualifying phrases it was also applied to the whole building (*"tent of meeting"* - Ex 29:4, 10, 42; Ex 40:34; etc.; *"tent of the testimony"* - Nu 9:15; 17:7; etc.) [8]

HOUSE

(Hebrew, *"bayith"* = house)

This word is applied to the whole tabernacle (Ex 23:19; 34:26; Js 6:24; etc.) It conveys the idea of a fixed habitation, and thus applied more correctly to the Tabernacle after the conquest of Canaan.

SANCTUARY

(Hebrew, *"miqdash"* = consecrated place)

It is used of the whole structure in Ex 25:8; Le 12:4; etc.; and sometimes only of the holy of holies (Le 16:2).

TEMPLE

(Hebrew, *"hekel"* = palace)

It is used of the tabernacle of Shiloh (1 Sa 1:9; 3:3), but more correctly later of the temple.

These words can now be summarised:

- Tabernacle = the inner covering; the framework; the whole building.

- Tent = the goat-hair covering; the whole building.

- House = the whole building.

- Sanctuary = the whole building; the holy of holies.

---

[8] Note: The AV rendering "tabernacle of the congregation" is based on the assumption that it was a place where the people met together. The central idea, however, is actually that of meeting <u>God</u> (Ex. 29:42; 30:6; etc.); hence "tent of meeting" is more accurate.

THE COMPONENTS OF THE TABERNACLE

THE TWO CURTAINS

There were four layers of material covering the tabernacle. The two inner layers were called *"curtains"*, and the two outer layers were called *"coverings"*. We will first examine the curtains.

- ### THE INNER CURTAIN

  See Ex 26:1-6; 36:8-13.

  The inner curtain lay immediately over the wooden frame of the tabernacle, and it was the only one visible from inside the building. It was, in fact, the walls and ceiling of the central sanctuary. In scripture it is always called the *"mishkan"*, that is, the *"tabernacle"* proper, for until it was secured in place the building was no more than a timber frame.

  The inner curtain was made of fine twined linen, interwoven with blue, purple, and scarlet threads, and embroidered with gold cherubim. It was intended to clothe the interior of the building with rich colour, beautiful design, and the awesome majesty of heaven.

  Ten curtains, each 28 cubits long and 4 cubits wide were joined to form two sections. Each of these sections was made of 5 curtains whose long sides were sewn together. The two sections were then united by means of 100 blue loops (50 on each section) and fifty gold clasps.

  When the inner curtain was in place, it fell short of the ground by one cubit on each side.

  You should also notice the three colours: **blue, purple,** and **scarlet**. They are always listed in that order; and they are found also at the outer gate, the door to the holy place, the veil, and the ephod of the high priest. The significance of these colours will be mentioned later.

Concerning **the cubit measure** used in the tabernacle, there are two main opinions: it may have been the official Egyptian royal cubit of 52.38 cm (20.625 inches); or it may have been the natural cubit (the length of a forearm measured to the tip of the middle finger) which was approximately 46 cm (18 inches). Because the royal cubit was a more precise measure and because Israel had just come out of Egypt, many commentators favour it as the probable unit of the length used in the tabernacle. An objection to this is that Solomon apparently used the shorter cubit as the standard measure for his temple (1 Kg 7:23-26; the capacity of the bronze laver indicates a cubit of 44. cm, or 17.5 inches).

- **THE SECOND CURTAIN, OR TENT**

See Ex 26:7-14; 36:14-19.

This curtain was made of goats' hair, and it was probably black (white goats were uncommon in Palestine in Bible days). It was called the *"tent"* because it was designed to fully cover and protect the inner curtain.

The tent was made of 11 pieces, sewn together in two groups of 5 and 6. Each of the 11 pieces measured 30 cubits x 4 cubits. When the two sections were joined together (by 100 loops and 50 bronze clasps) the full curtain then measured 30 x 44 cubits.

The tent was so arranged that on three sides it just touched the ground, while the excess length of the curtain allowed a kind of gable or porch to be formed at the front. In the opinion of Josephus it was a gable:

"(the tent curtains) were woven with hair, with the like subtlety as those of wool were made, and were extended loosely down to the ground, **appearing like a triangular front and elevation at the gates . .**"

THE TWO COVERINGS

These were made of more durable material than the two curtains, and they provided adequate protection from the weather for the tabernacle and its other furnishings.

Josephus describes them thus -

> There were also other curtains made of skins above these, which afforded covering and protection to those that were woven, both in hot weather and when it rained; and great was the surprise of those who viewed these curtains at a distance, for they seemed not at all to differ from the colour of the sky; but those that were made of hair and of skins, reached down in the same manner as did the veil at the gates, and kept off the heat of the sun, and what injury the rains might do . . . [9]

Almost everything we know about these coverings is contained in just two verses:

> "Make for the tent a covering of ram skins dyed red, and over that a covering of hides of sea cows . . . Then they made for the tent a covering of ram skins dyed red, and over that a covering of hides of sea cows *(Ex 26:14; 36:19 NIV. Note that the "tanned rams' skins" of the REV is not strong enough.)*

---

[9] Op. cit. Book 3, ch. 6.

The Hebrew word translates "sea cows" actually refers to an animal whose identity is now unknown. It was certainly not a badger (as stated in the AV); it may have been a Red Sea dugong. A number of ancient versions took the word to refer to a colour, usually a deep blue - so the Vulgate and the LXX read, *"skins dyed a violet colour"*. Josephus, in the quote given above, obviously thought the same: "great was the surprise of those who viewed these curtains at a distance, for they seemed not at all to differ from the colour of the sky." However, modern commentators disallow this ancient view, and the general consensus is some kind of sea animal which would provide a durable and water-proof skin.

No dimensions are given for the two outer coverings, but they were presumably similar in size to the tent.

THE FRAMEWORK

See Ex 26:15-20; 36:20-34.

The basic structure of the tabernacle was made of timber, in the form of 46 upright frames, each 10 x 1.5 cubits. These frames were set in silver sockets, 20 on each side, and 6 at the western end with 2 corner frames. The sides were thus each 30 cubits long. The ends were 9 cubits, plus the corner frames, which evidently made a total width of 10 cubits. The dimensions of the full building were therefore 30 x 10 x 10 cubits. The eastern end, facing sunrise, was left open.

The frames were joined by cross bars, 5 for each wall, with the middle one *"passing through from end to end."* The frames and bars were all overlaid with gold.

Much debate surrounds these frames, especially about their construction and their spiritual meaning -

- **CONSTRUCTION**

Were they frames or boards; how were they locked together; how were the bars placed? - and so on. The information given in Exodus is imprecise.

Some translations and commentators prefer to use the word *"boards"* instead of *"frames"* (as in the RSV), and they argue that these boards were locked together to form a continuous unbroken wall. Josephus thought this was the case:

> There were also pillars made of wood, twenty on each side; they were wrought into a quadrangular figure, in breadth a cubit and a half, but the thickness was four fingers: they had thin plates of gold affixed to them on both sides, inwardly and outwardly: they had each of them two tenons belonging to them, inserted into their bases, and these were of silver, in each of which bases there was a socket to receive the tenons; but the pillars on the west wall were six. Now all these tenons and sockets accurately fitted one another, insomuch that the joints were invisible, and both seemed to be one entire and united wall. It was also covered with gold, both within and without . . . Now every one of the pillars had rings of gold affixed to their fronts outward, as if they had taken root in the pillars . . . through which were inserted bars gilt over with gold . . . being so fastened in their joints that they held the whole firmly together; and for this reason was all this joined so fast together, that the tabernacle might not

be shaken, either by the winds, or by any
other leans, but that it might preserve
itself quiet and immovable continually.
(Op. cit.)

There are two arguments in favour of open frames rather
than boards: the great weight of boards, which would
severely lessen the portability of the tabernacle; and a solid
wall would hide the beautiful inner curtain, except for the
ceiling. For these reasons, and perhaps others also, most
recent translations prefer *"frames"* (RSV, NIV, GNB, MLB,
etc.).

- **INTERPRETATION**

  Marvellous ingenuity has been expended to invent [10] a
  spiritual symbolism for the boards, sockets, rings, and
  bars. Deep lessons are drawn from the fact that the
  wood was acacia, that it came from trees which first
  had to be cut **down**, then cut **up**, then polished, then
  plated with gold! Then how could anyone miss the
  significance of the silver sockets that were driven into
  the sand, and that there were two of them for each
  frame, and that the frames were locked together,
  "shoulder to shoulder", standing brave and tall against
  the desert storms? Did you not realise that these
  sockets were **in** the desert yet they were not **of** it, and
  that they separated the boards, which had once (as
  trees) been rooted in the sand, from the sand? And
  what a wealth of revelation can be extracted from the
  number of the frames, and from their dimensions, and
  from the rings and bars which held them together.
  And even then we have hardly begun to explore the
  possibilities!

---

[10] I do not apologise for the word. Almost all detailed application of the
tabernacle types lack any specific biblical warrant. They are based on
imagination (albeit sanctified), and cannot claim any final authority.

Now I am not saying that such a use of tabernacle typology is wrong, only that it has little biblical authority. It depends more on imagination than revelation. These notes will not be entirely guiltless of such symbolism; but in general they will look for a broadly based typology, rather than for detailed application. The pursuit of exact analogies is no doubt a fascinating quest, but I would prefer to keep to interpretations for which there is some solid scriptural support. [11]

ERECTION

See Ex 26:12-13; 40:17-33.

When the framework was erected, the inner curtain was thrown over it lengthwise, so that its 40 cubits covered the top and the western (rear) wall (a total of 30 + 10 cubits), with perhaps a cubit draped over the front, so that only the corners touched the ground at the back.

The inner curtain also draped against the two side walls, falling short of the ground by one cubit, for its 28 cubits were 2 cubits less than the total of 30 needed to cover fully the roof and the two side walls.

The tent was then draped over the inner curtain, so that its edges did touch the ground on three sides, and the surplus

---

[11] The three books by Slemming, mentioned earlier, offer detailed and frequently delightful applications of every aspect of the tabernacle, all of them in harmony with NT teaching - that is Slemming does not use any type to teach anything other than what is clearly taught in the NT. Although I have no personal interest in searching out a meaning for every detail of the tabernacle, I have no quarrel with those who do, and I admire their creativity, so long as they do not depart from sound doctrine. Typology becomes harmful only when it begins to formulate doctrine in its own right, without clear support from other plainer parts of scripture.

length at the front was arranged (as I have indicated above) to form either a porch or a gable, or perhaps merely a fringe.

The other two coverings were then added: first the red skin covering; and then the (blue?) water-proof covering.

The roof was thus flat, there being no ridge pole. There have been attempts from time to time to prove that the tabernacle must have had a ridge pole, and that the *"tent"* was indeed pitched over the whole structure in the ordinary gable shape. None of these attempts has been fully successful, and the consensus remains that the tabernacle had a flat roof.

Once all of the coverings were in place, the embroidered inner curtain was visible only from the inside.

THE VEIL AND SCREEN

See Ex 26:31-37; 36:35-38.

Twenty cubits from the eastern end of the sanctuary a veil was erected, made of fine twined linen interwoven with blue, purple, and scarlet threads, and embroidered with cherubim. Thus it was identical with the inner curtain. This veil divided the sanctuary into two rooms: the first, 20 x 10 cubits, lay to the east of the veil, and it was called *"the holy place"*. The veil was hung upon four pillars made of acacia wood overlaid with gold. Golden hooks and clasps were used, and the pillars stood in silver sockets which were driven into the sand.

On the western side of the veil a smaller room was formed called *"the most holy place"*, or *"the holy of holies"* (He 9:3), or *"the holiest of all"* (He 9:3, AV). [12]

Although no dimensions are given, it is normally thought that the holy of holies was a cube of 10 cubits. This is

---

[12] Note that in He. 9:12, 25 the title "Holy Place" is used to designate the holy of holies.

confirmed by Solomon's temple, which was twice the length and breadth of the tabernacle, and in which the holy of holies was a cube of 20 cubits (1 Kg 6:2, 20).

Across the open eastern end of the sanctuary five acacia wood pillars were placed, overlaid with gold, standing on bronze bases, and providing support for the screen which formed the door into the holy place. Like the veil and the inner curtain, this screen was made of fine twined linen, interwoven with blue, and purple and scarlet, and intricately embroidered. However, it seems that cherubim were not included in the pattern of this embroidery. These heavenly beings were located only inside the sanctuary, out of sight of all but the priests.

THE OUTER COURT

See Ex 27:9-18; 38:9-20.

The outer court was a large open rectangular area, measuring 100 x 50 cubits. This was surrounded by a fence five cubits high. The fence was made of plain linen, suspended by silver hooks and fillets from posts that were 20 pillars along each side of the court, and 10 pillars at each end (notice that no adjustment is made in Exodus for the doubling up of the pillars at the four corners).

At the eastern end, the four central spaces between the pillars were left for an entrance, and this gateway was then screened by a curtain of fine linen identical to that used for the entrance to the sanctuary.

The fence was supported by cords fastened to bronze pegs which were probably driven into the earth on both sides of the boundary. Ex 38:20 indicates that similar pegs and cords were also used to strengthen the tabernacle.

THE CONTENTS OF THE TABERNACLE

The tabernacle contained the following articles -

IN THE OUTER COURT

- ### THE ALTAR OF BURNT OFFERINGS

  See pages 5 & 6; and Ex 27:1-8; 38:1-7.

  This was also called the bronze altar (Ex 39:39); or the table of the Lord (Ma 1:7, 12); or the altar of the Lord your God (De 12:27) and perhaps it had still other names.

  The bronze altar was located a short distance inside the entrance to the outer court. It was made of acacia wood overlaid with bronze, three cubits high, and five cubits square. There were horns on each corner, to which the sacrifices were secured, and it was equipped also with a grating and carrying poles.

  Several bronze utensils were supplied for use at the altar - ashpans, basins, forks, firepans, and shovels.

  Josephus describes it thus -

  > Before this tabernacle there was reared a brazen altar, but it was within made of wood . . . adorned with brass plates, as bright as gold. It had also a brazen hearth of net-work; for the ground underneath received the fire from the heart, because it had no basis to receive it. Hard by this altar lay the basins, and the vials, and the censers, and the caldrons, made of gold; but the other vessels, made for the use of the sacrifices, were all of brass. (Op. cit.)

This description confirms what is now a widely held view that the altar was quite hollow, lacking even a floor. When it was set in place it was filled with earth or stones, thus creating a bed for the fire, and a platform on which to lay various animal sacrifices and burnt offerings.

Halfway up the altar, on the outside, was a ledge, perhaps as much as a cubit broad, which extended completely around it, thus providing a platform on which the officiating priest could stand (remember that the altar may have been nearly 160 cm. high, 62 inches). The bronze grating (or net) probably acted as a support for this ledge, so it was not a grate in the ordinary sense of the word; that is, it did not carry the fire. Four rings were fixed to the grating, through which the bronze-covered acacia wood carrying poles were thrust.

- **THE LAVER**

See Ex 30:17-21; 38:8.

No details are given of the dimensions or shape of the laver. Most commentators assume that it was a large round bowl, set on a circular base, all made of bronze. Because of the special notice which is always taken of the **base** (30:18; 31:9; 35:16; 39:39; 40:11; Le 8:11), some writers suggest that it may have been a kind of separate trough into which smaller quantities of water were drawn from the laver. In this way the officiating priests would use only as much water as they needed without spoiling the main supply.

Solomon built his temple on a scale double that of the ancient tabernacle, and his laver had a diameter of ten cubits, which may indicate a diameter of 5 cubits for the original laver (1 Kg 7:23).

The metal for the laver came from bronze mirrors donated by *"the ministering women who ministered at the door of the tent of meeting"* (38:8).

> According to 1 Sa 2:22 . . . (these were) women who dedicated their lives to the service of Jehovah, and spent them in religious exercises, in fasting and in prayer, like Anna, the daughter of Phanuel, mentioned in Lu 2:37 . . . The mirrors of the women had been used for the purpose of earthly adorning. But now the pious Israelites renounced this earthly adorning, and offered it to the Lord as a heave-offering to make the purifying laver in front of the sanctuary, in order that "what had hitherto served as a means of procuring applause in the world might henceforth be the means of procuring the approbation of God" . . . The laver was to be placed between the tabernacle . . .and the altar in the court (vs.18), probably not in a straight line with the door of the dwelling and the altar of burnt-offering, but more sideways, so as to be convenient for the use of the priests, whether they were going into the tabernacle, or going up to the altar for service, to kindle a firing for Jehovah, i.e. to offer sacrifice upon the altar. They were to wash their hands, with which they touched the holy things, and their feet, with which they trod the holy ground (see 3:5), "that they might not die," as is again emphatically stated in vs. 20 and 21. For touching the holy things with unclean hands, and treading

upon the floor of the sanctuary with dirty feet, would have been a sin against Jehovah, the Holy One of Israel, deserving of death. [13]

The laver is the only part of the tabernacle for which no transportation details are given.

IN THE HOLY PLACE

- ### THE TABLE OF SHOWBREAD

See pages 5 & 6; and Ex 25:23-30; 37:10-16.

The Hebrew name of this table means *"table of the face"*; it is also called *"the table of the bread of the Presence"* (25:30). Josephus describes it thus:

But in the holy place he placed a table, like those at Delphi: its length was two cubits, and its breadth one cubit, and its height three spans. It had feet also, the lower half of which were complete feet, resembling those which the Dorians put to their bedsteads; but the upper parts towards the table were wrought into square form. The table has a hollow towards every side, having a ledge of four fingers' depth, that went around like a spiral, both on the upper and lower part of the body of the work. Upon every one of the feet was there also inserted a ring, not far from the cover, through which went bars of wood beneath, but gilded, to be taken out

---

[13] Keil and Delitzsch, <u>Commentary on the Old Testament</u>, Vol. 1, The Pentateuch, Vol. 2, pg. 213, 214. Eerdmans Pub. Co, Grand Rapids, Michigan; 1976 reprint.

upon occasion. and by these it was carried when they journeyed. Upon this table, which was placed on the north side of the temple, not far from the most holy place, were laid twelve unleavened loaves of bread, six upon each heap, one above another . . . and above these loaves were put two vials full of frankincense. (Op. cit.)

The table was made of acacia wood, covered with pure beaten gold, and girded by two ornamental golden wreaths, or crowns, one inside the other. The vessels used on the table were all made of pure gold - large deep plates for the bread; bowls and spoons for incense; flagons, bowls and goblets for wine libations.

An incense altar from the ancient Near East. 1200 - 1100 BC

The loaves were called *"the bread of the face"* because they stood on the table before the face of the Lord as an offering from the people of Israel. Other names are: *"bread of the Presence"* (Ex 25:30); *"the continual bread"* (1 Ch 9:32, lit.); *"show-bread"* (He 9:2; the Greek word = *"the presentation bread"*). The significance of the showbread is not explained in scripture, but it probably represented such ideas as:

– Man is utterly dependent on God as his Provider.

– Man must offer back to God all of his labour.

– The twelve tribes of Israel (figured in the twelve loaves) were always under the watchful eye of Jehovah.

– The whole nation (symbolised by the loaves) dwelt in the holy place, and they were all priests before God.

Each Sabbath the stale loaves were removed and given to the priests, and fresh bread was placed on the table (1 Ch 9:32; 1 Sa 21:6).

As Josephus says, and as Moses commanded, the table of showbread stood on the north side of the holy place, that is, on the right hand side as one entered the sanctuary (Ex 26:35). The golden double moulding probably had two functions (apart from beauty): firstly, to prevent the utensils and bread from falling: secondly, to separate the utensils (which were probably placed on the outer shelf, between the mouldings) from the bread (which presumably was placed on two golden platters in the centre of the table). Scripture itself offers no explanation of these matters.

- **THE LAMPSTAND**

  See Ex 25:31-39; 37:17-24.

  The Hebrew word is *"menorah"* = lampstand (incorrectly called a candlestick in the AV).

  The lampstand stood on the south side of the holy place (that is, on the left hand as one entered the sanctuary). No indication of its size is given in scripture, except that a "talent" (34 kg or 75 lb) of pure gold had to be used in its manufacture. However, a bas-relief on the Arch of Titus in Rome suggests that it may have been about 3.5 cubits high and about 2 cubits wide (see illustrations on pages 5 & 6 and also the next paragraph).

  Despite the lack of information about its size, scripture does provide a detailed description of its appearance. It had a central shaft, on each side of which were three branches. These branches are usually pictured as curved, as they are in the lampstand on the Arch of Titus. However, because of suspected non-Jewish figures on that lampstand some scholars doubt that it could have been taken from Herod's temple, and there are other reasons to believe that the branches of the original lampstand may in fact have been straight, not curved. Most scholars agree that the actual lamps and flames were probably all at the same level (as shown in the illustration).

  Whether or not the lamps burned continually, or were extinguished each morning and rekindled each evening remains uncertain - cp. Ex 30:7-8 with 1 Sa 3:3. Golden snuffers, trays, and other utensils were made for use with the lamps.

  The design of each of the seven parts of the lampstand included a series of "almond-shaped cups, capitals, and flowers". This probably means a series of shapes, the first of which was elongated, the second globular, and the third like a blossoming bud. There were three of each of these groups on each branch, and four groups on the central shaft - thus making a total of 66 ornaments, but somehow Josephus managed to count 70 -

> . . . near the southern wall was set a candle-stick of cast gold, hollow within, being of the weight of one hundred pounds . It was made with its knops, and lilies, and pomegranates, and bowls (which ornaments amounted to 70 in all;) by which means the shaft elevated itself on high from a single base, and spread itself into as many branches as there are planets, including the sun among them. It terminated in seven heads, in one row, all standing parallel to one another; and these branches carried seven lamps, one by one, in imitation of the number of the planets. These lamps looked to the east and to the south, the candlestick being situated obliquely. (Op. cit.).

• THE ALTAR OF INCENSE

See the illustration above; and Ex 30:1-10; 37:25-28.

> Now between (the) candlestick and the table, which, as we said, were within the sanctuary, was the altar of incense, made of wood indeed, but of the same wood of which the (other) vessels were made, such as was not liable to corruption; it was entirely crusted over with a golden plate. Its breadth on each

side was a cubit, but the altitude double. Upon it was a grate of gold, that was extant above the altar, which had a golden crown encompassing it round about, where to belonged rings and bars, by which the priests carried it when they journeyed. (Josephus, op. cit.).

Josephus forgot to mention that this altar also had four horns, placed one on each corner. Because it was completely overlaid with pure gold, the altar of incense was also known as the *"golden altar"* (Ex 39:38; 40:4, 26; Nu 4:11).

The altar of incense was placed directly in front of the Ark of the Covenant, being separated from it only by the great veil. Special emphasis was placed on this location (cp. Ex 30:6), and this proximity to the ark sometimes caused people to think of the golden altar as belonging to the holy of holies more than to the holy place (1 Kg 6:22; He 9:4).

Once a year, on the great day of atonement, the high priest sprinkled upon its horns the blood of the sin offering (Ex 30:6-10; Le 16:18-19). Also, every morning and evening, incense was burnt on it with fire taken from the altar of burnt offering. Nadab and Abihu, perhaps under intoxication, were struck dead because they used *"unholy fire"* (that is, fire not taken from the altar of burnt offering) to burn incense on the golden altar (Le 10:1-3).

The altar of incense is usually thought to symbolise in various ways the prayers of the people, and their right of access through prayer to the throne of God in heaven.

IN THE HOLY OF HOLIES

Only one article of furniture stood in the holiest place, and that was the ark of the covenant of the Lord (Ex 25:10-22; 37:1-9).

- Moses was given more precise instructions for this piece of furniture than for any other part of the tabernacle, and it was also the beginning of the pattern God showed him on Sinai. The Lord had said -

  Let them make me a sanctuary, that I may dwell in their midst. According to all that I show you concerning the pattern of the tabernacle, and all of its furniture, so you shall make it (Ex 25:8-9).

  It might be expected that the Lord would then have begun to describe the outer fence, or certainly the sanctuary; but no, his next words were: *"They shall make an ark of acacia wood . . ." (vs. 10).*

  Slemming comments -

  > We usually choose the furniture according to the building, but not so with the Lord. He commences where he always does, at the heart of things, working from within to without (op. cit., pg. 125).

- Many titles were given to the ark, including the following: ark of the Lord (Js 4:11); ark of God (1 Sa 3:3); holy ark (2 Ch 35:3); ark of thy might (Ps 132:8). It was a chest made of gold-covered acacia wood, 2.5 cubits long, 1.5 cubits wide, and 1.5 cubits high. For carrying purposes it was equipped with four *"feet"*, four gold rings, and two gold-covered poles. Round about the ark there was a golden rim, or moulding, encircling it like an ornamental wreath.

A lid or covering was placed on the ark, called in Hebrew a *"capporeth"* = an atoning covering, commonly called in English the "mercy seat". This was actually the most important part of the ark; indeed it gave its name to the most holy place - *"the room for the mercy seat"* (1 Ch 28:11). Unlike the ark, the mercy seat was not made of timber overlaid with gold, but it was fashioned out of pure gold, with two cherubim formed upon its top. The cherubim were not merely added to the mercy seat, but were formed out of the same piece of gold, so that they were an integral and inseparable part of the mercy seat.

The appearance of the cherubim is uncertain. They may have been fully human in form, or perhaps may have been shaped like the hybrid winged creatures that were common in Bible lands. Even Josephus was unsure about their shape -

> Upon this its cover were two images, which the Hebrews call cherubim; they are flying creatures, but their form is not like to that of any of the creatures which men have seen, though Moses said he had seen such beings near the throne of God (op. cit.).

Whatever form the cherubim had, it does seem probable that they were not kneeling as they are often portrayed, but standing (2 Ch 3:13).

> Standing upon the "capporeth" . . . with their wings outspread and faces towered, they represented the spirits of heaven, who surround Jehovah, the heavenly King, when seated upon his

throne, as his most exalted servants and the witnesses of his sovereignty and saving glory; so that Jehovah enthroned above the wings of the cherubim was set forth as the God of Hosts who is exalted above all the angels, surrounded by the assembly or council of the holy ones (Ps 89:6-9), who bow their faces toward the "capporeth", studying the secrets of the divine counsels of love (1 Pe 1:12), and worshipping him that lives for ever and ever (Re 4:10). [14]

- The mercy seat had a double significance. **First**, it was the place where God and Israel met together on earth. The Lord promised to appear in a cloud above the mercy seat (Ex 25:22; Le 16:2). This cloud is often referred to as the "*shekinah*" = the presence (of God), but this Hebrew word does not appear in the OT. It was however a favourite expression of the rabbis and from the beginning was adopted by the church. **Second**, the mercy seat was the place of atonement, but this will be discussed later.

- Inside the Ark of the Covenant were placed

  - The two tablets of stone on which the commandments were written (He 9:4; De 31:26; 1 Kg 8:9). With doubtful plausibility, Josephus says "the commandments were written, five upon each table, and two and a half upon each side of them."

  - An urn of manna (He 9:4; Ex. 16:33-34).

---

[14] Keil and Delitzsch, op. cit., pg. 170. See also 1 Sam. 4:4; 2 Sam 6:2; Ps. 80:2.

    – Aaron's rod that budded (He 9:4; Nu 17:10).

THE GARMENTS OF THE HIGH PRIEST

See Exodus chapter 28, and the drawing below.

Special holy garments were provided for Aaron, the first high priest, *"for glory and for beauty"* (vs. 2.). "The quality of the whole of these vestments, whether it was texture or material or workmanship, was the very best of its kind - **fine** linen, **pure** gold, **precious** stones, **costly** ointment, **cunning** workmanship, all used by **wise** hearts. This was because it was all a type of Christ's character, and nothing but the very highest quality will do to portray him who was an example of humanity as it ought to be and as one day it will be. Jesus was Divinity manifested in humanity so that humanity might take on Divinity by becoming the sons of God . . . Humanity and Divinity harmonised only in the High Priest of our profession. [15]

THE EPHOD

See Ex 28:5-14; 39:2-7.

An ephod was simply a loin cloth (1 Sa 2:18; 2 Sa 6:14, 20). It was a distinctive part of every priest's clothing (1 Sa 22:18). In the case of the high priest, it may have taken the form of an apron. It was suspended on shoulder straps and coloured gold, blue, purple, and scarlet (Ex 28:6-7). On the shoulder straps were two onyx stones, set in gold, each bearing the names of *"six of the sons of Israel"*. Gold chains were also attached to the ephod, presumably to support the breast piece (vs. 13-14, 27-28).

---

[15] Slemming, <u>These are the Garments</u>, pg. 27.

THE BREAST PIECE

See Ex 28:15-30; 39:8-21.

This was a piece of linen, interwoven with gold, blue, purple, and scarlet colours, about 23 cm. square, and folded double, apparently to form a bag (vs. 15-16). Mounted on the breast piece were twelve precious stones, set in four rows of three, each stone representing one of the twelve tribes. This symbolised the high priest's function as representative of the people of Israel before the Lord (28:29).

The breast piece was attached by gold chains to the shoulder pieces of the ephod.

THE URIM AND THUMMIM

See Ex 28:30.

- Curiosity abounds about these mysterious objects, but their real nature remains as much a mystery today as it had already become long before the time of Christ. Even the meaning of the words is uncertain.

  However, it is clear that the Urim and Thummim were used for obtaining divine guidance or for ascertaining the will of God.

  Thus, Joshua was to seek the Lord's guidance *"by the judgment of the Urim"* (Nu 27:21); Saul used it to discover Jonathan's guilt (1 Sa 14:41-42, REV but not AV); David used the ephod, presumably because the Urim and Thummim were with it (1 Sa 23:6-14). On the other hand, Saul got no answer - either from a dream, or from the Urim, or from a prophet (1 Sa 28:6).

  "Urim" may mean either *"lights"* or *"curses"*; and *"Thummim"* probably means *"perfections"*. If the combined meaning is *"lights and perfections"*, then

the idea is one of perfect guidance; but if the meaning is *"curses and perfections"*, then the idea is that the matter under question will receive either God's curse or his blessing. But the words may originally have had altogether different meanings, which have long since been lost.

Aaron, the High Priest

- There are two main ideas about how the Urim and Thummim were used -

  ### - THE ANCIENT VIEW

  Some read Ex 28:30 this way: *"You shall put upon the* oracle *of judgment the Urim and Thummim."* This suggests that the twelve jewels on the breast piece were the Urim and Thummim, and that in a manner nowhere described in scripture these stones were able to serve as divine oracles.

Many of the ancients thought that a supernatural light shone from one or more of the jewels and thus revealed the mind of God (a belief that may have arisen from interpreting Urim as "lights").

Josephus reckoned that the breast piece was itself the Urim and Thummim, and he was sure that not only those twelve jewels shone with a divine radiance, but also the onyx stones on the shoulders of the high priest -

For as to those stones which . . . the high priest bare on his shoulders, which were sardonyxes . . . the one of them shined out when God was present at their sacrifices . . . bright rays darting out thence, and being seen even by those that were most remote; which splendour yet was not before natural to the stone . Yet I will mention what is still more wonderful than this: for God declared beforehand, by those twelve stones which the high priest bare on his breast, and which were inserted into his breastplate . . . for so great a splendour shone forth from them . . . that all the people were sensible of God's being present for their assistance . . . Whence it came to pass that those Greeks . . . because they could not possibly contradict this, called that breast plate "the Oracle". [16]

Few if any scholars would now give credence to the idea that a supernatural light shone from the stones; but some would still allow that the

---

[16] Op. Cit. ch. 8, #9.

breast piece (or perhaps only its twelve jewels) was itself the Urim and Thummim.

– A BETTER VIEW

The more widely accepted view is that the Urim and Thummim were two stones, perhaps gems, which were distinguishable in some way - perhaps by colour, size, or specific marks. These two stones were kept in the pouch formed by the folded cloth of the breast piece, and when divine counsel was needed they were either cast or drawn from the pouch (if drawn out, they must have been identical in size and shape). Whether drawn or cast the stones were able to provide three responses: "Yes", "No", and "No answer" (or perhaps, "Cursing", "Blessing", "No answer") - see again 1 Sa 14:41; also 23:6ff where all of David's questions may be answered with a simple "Yes" or "No"; and cp. Pr 16:33, which may refer to (or include) the act of tossing the Urim and Thummim from the pouch into the lap of the priest.

- By the time of Nehemiah, if not long before, the Urim and Thummim no longer existed in Israel (Ezr 2:63; Ne 7:65). The reason for this disappearance is not given in scripture. Josephus, however, added another few centuries to their use, and also offered a reason for their cessation: "Now this breastplate, and this sardonyx, left off shining two hundred years before I composed this book (Ad 93/94), God having been displeased at the transgressions of his laws" (op. cit.).

- For many years a hope was entertained among the pious that God would restore the Urim and Thummim to Israel: "Nehemiah the governor told them that they should not participate in the sacred offerings until a high priest arose wearing the breast piece of Revelation and Truth" . . . "The Jews and their priests confirmed Simon as their leader and high priest in perpetuity until a true prophet (that is, one with Urim and Thummim) should appear" (1 Es 5:40; 1 Mc. 14:41; and cp. Ne 7:65; 1 Mc. 4:46).

But the more thoughtful rabbis turned their interest away from such extraordinary means of gaining Divine counsel, and turned instead to the law of God. There is little doubt that this was a step towards spiritual maturity, and that these rabbis were correct in supposing that God would never again restore the Urim and Thummim. They spoke with respect about the ancient ways -

> God robed Aaron in perfect splendour, and armed him with the emblems of power . . . He gave him the sacred vestment adorned by an embroiderer with gold and violet and purple; **The oracle of judgment with the tokens of truth** (that is, the breast piece with Urim and Thummim) . . . What rich adornments to feast the eyes! What a miracle of art! What a proud honour!"

Nonetheless, the same rabbi was certain that the man who possessed and loved the whole law of God held in his hand an oracle better than Aaron ever knew -

> Disaster never comes the way of the man who fears the Lord: in times of trial he will be rescued again and again . . . A sensible man trusts the law and finds it as reliable as the divine oracle. (Sir 45:8, 10, 33:1-3; NEB).

THE ROBE

See Ex 28:31-35; 39:22-26.

Immediately under the ephod, the high priest wore a blue robe, and around its hem was a row of pomegranates and gold bells. The bells were real, and were intended to bear witness to the people listening outside the sanctuary that the high priest was moving around inside and fulfilling his duties. So long as the people could hear the bells they knew that the high priest had duly sanctified himself to enter the presence of God, and that he had been accepted by the Lord. If the bells fell silent it would indicate that the priest had been judged unclean and had been stricken by God (vs. 35).

It is uncertain whether the pomegranates were merely embroidered on the cloth, or whether they were actual globes, shaped like pomegranates, and dangling between each pair of bells. The pomegranates were coloured blue, purple, and scarlet.

THE TURBAN

See Ex 28:36-38; 39:30-31.

A linen turban was wound around the high priest's head, and a gold plate was fixed to the front of it by ribbons of blue lace. The plate bore the words, *"Holy to the Lord"*.

THE COAT

See Ex 28:39; 39:27.

Under the robe, the high priest wore a fine linen coat, woven in checker work, and provided with a girdle.

THE BREECHES

See Ex 28:42; 39:27-29.

The final item of dress (although the first to be put on) was a pair of linen breeches which reached from the loins to the thighs.

All told there were eight specific articles of clothing. Four of them were worn by all priests: the breeches the coat, the girdle, and the turban. Four of them were worn only by the high priest: the blue robe, the ephod with its girdle, the breast piece, and the special high-priestly turban.

It should be noticed also that priests were forbidden to wear woollen garments, and they had to go barefoot when they were inside the sanctuary (Ez 44:17; Ex 3:5; 29:20).

CARING FOR THE TABERNACLE

The tabernacle had to be dismantled and re-erected during the travels of Israel (1 Ch 17:5-6). Certain families from the tribe of Levi were given various duties to fulfil within the tabernacle, and also responsibility for its care and transport - see Nu 1:47ff. Duties were assigned as follows -

THE FAMILY OF GERSHON

See Nu 3:21-26.

- The inner curtain, the tent, the screen, the courtyard hangings and gate screen, the cords.

THE FAMILY OF KOHATH

See Nu 3:27-32.

- The ark, the table, the lampstand, the altars, the vessels, the veil. These furnishings had to be covered in transit (see Nu 4:1 ff). They were covered as follows -

  - the ark: the veil, a blue cloth, a goatskin

- the table: a blue cloth

- The vessels and bread: a scarlet cloth, a goatskin.

- The lampstand: a blue cloth, in a covering of goatskin, on a carrying frame.

- The altar of incense: a blue cloth, a goatskin.

- The vessels: a blue-cloth in a covering of goatskin on a carrying frame.

- The altar: a purple cloth.

- The altar utensils: on the altar, a goatskin.

During transit, none of these items was to have been touched by hand. Everything had to be properly placed in position, covered, and then carefully carried either by means of the special carrying poles, or by carrying frames.

THE FAMILY OF MERARI

See Nu 3:33-37.

- The tabernacle wall frames, the bars, the pillars, the bases, the pegs, and cords.

  Whenever the procession bearing the ark began to move, Moses would cry:

  Arise, O Lord, and let they enemies be scattered; and let them that hate thee flee before thee!

  And when the ark came to rest, he would say:

  Return, O Lord, to the ten thousand thousands of Israel! (Nu 10:33-36; Ps 68:1; 132:8).

WHERE WAS THE TABERNACLE PLACED?

The tabernacle had to be placed in the centre of the camp, with the tribes arrayed around it in a set pattern. According to Numbers chapter one, the arrangement was as follows –

MANASSEH EPHRAIM BENJAMIN

LEVITES GERSHONITES

SIMEON REUBEN GAD
LEVITES . KOHATHITES

ASHER DAN NAPHTALI
LEVITES . MERARITES

MOSES. AARON. PRIESTS

ISSACHAR JUDAH ZEBULUN

WHAT HAPPENED TO THE TABERNACLE?

When it was first erected the tabernacle was covered by a column of cloud by day, and of fire by night (Nu 9:15-16). The movement of this column guided the people during their journeyings through the wilderness. When the cloud settled they encamped (9:17). Details of these movements are given in Nu 9:18-23; 10:11-36; 14:14).

The Ark of the Covenant was carried by the priests to the Jordan. When their feet touched the water, the river was divided, and the people were able to walk across to the other side (Js 3:13-17). The ark also preceded the marchers around Jericho (Js 6:8).

Eventually the tabernacle was set up at Shiloh, about 25 miles north of Jerusalem (Js 18:1), where it was still to be found 250 years later in the days of Samuel. By this time it seems to have been made into a more substantial building (cp. 1 Sa 1:3; 3:15).

In a desperate effort to defeat the Philistines, Israel brought the ark into battle, but they were still defeated, and the ark was placed in the Philistine temple of Dagon (1 Sa 4:1 ff.). However, it brought the Philistines so much misfortune that they returned it to Israel, and it was lodged in a house at Kiriath-Jearim where it remained for 20 years (1 Sa 7:2). It is possible that during the time the Philistines had possession of the ark Aaron's rod and the pot of manna may have been lost; at least, when the ark finally came to rest in Solomon's temple it then contained only the slabs of stone on which the Decalogue was carved (1 Kg 8:9).

David sought to bring the ark from Kiriath-Jearim to Jerusalem, but on the death of Uzziah left it at the house of Obed-Edom for three months (2 Sa 6:1 ff.). David then brought the ark to Jerusalem and erected a tent for it there (vs. 17). The tabernacle itself may have been destroyed by the Philistines, and thus had had to be rebuilt. In any case, by this time it was no longer at Shiloh, but at Gibeon, about 10 miles north of Jerusalem (1 Ch 16:39-42; 21:29 2 Ch 1:3-4).

Ultimately, both David's tent and the tabernacle were replaced by Solomon's temple (2 Ch 5:1ff), which was patterned on the tabernacle design.

The last biblical reference to the ark is in 2 Ch 35:3, where it is recorded that King Josiah had it restored to its proper place in the temple. However, a passage in the Apocrypha adds -

> . . . this document records that, prompted by a divine message, the prophet (Jeremiah) gave orders that the Tent of Meeting and the ark should go with him. Then he went away to the mountain from the top of which Moses saw God's promised land. When he reached the mountain, Jeremiah found a cave dwelling; he carried the tent, the ark, and the incense-altar into it, then blocked up the entrance. Some of his companions came to mark out the way, but were unable to find it. "The place shall remain unknown," he said, "until God finally gathers his people together and shows mercy to them. Then the Lord will bring these things to light again, and the glory of the Lord will appear with the cloud, as it was seen both in the time of Moses and when Solomon prayed that the shrine might be worthily consecrated." (2 Mc 2:4-8, NEB)

CHAPTER TWO

TYPES AND SHADOWS

INTRODUCTION

For anyone who takes the message of the Bible seriously it is obvious that Israel's ancient tabernacle is far more than an historical curiosity. The number of chapters devoted to the structure and to its ceremonies, the detailed descriptions that are given, the fearful penalties attached to even small violations of the ritual, the central place occupied by the tabernacle in the corporate life of the nation and in the religious experience of each citizen, all indicate its vital spiritual significance As surely as it once had this deep meaning for the nation, so now it has an important message for the church.

But how should that message be interpreted? And how important is it? Widely different answers are given to those two questions.

There are those who are fascinated by every detail of the sanctuary, its furniture, and its ordinances. Nothing is too small to escape their attention. Everything is accorded some kind of spiritual significance - every board, thread, embroidery, socket, cloth, cover, cord, vessel, furnishing, garment, tassel, ceremony, rule and regulation - nothing is without meaning, everything can be applied to some aspect of modern faith and worship.

There are those who give a revelatory and eschatological significance to the tabernacle. They not only see it as an illustration of things that are taught in the NT, but they use it in the present, and in the future. Around the tabernacle and its types they build entire systems of doctrine, they construct ideas and beliefs, of which no real indication is given elsewhere in scripture.

Then there are those (including your present author) who find the study of the tabernacle deeply interesting, but who allow their study of it be restrained by the following factors

- The information given in scripture about the tabernacle is frequently inadequate, and any modern reconstruction must rely at many points on conjecture - certainty is just not possible about the final design, appearance, and placement of all the parts of the building, its coverings, furniture, utensils, etc.

- While the broad outlines of the tabernacle and its ceremonies are clear enough, and they can be related with confidence to various aspects of the gospel, there is no such consensus about applying the details. Opinions are legion as to the meanings to be given to each small part. All of these opinions must remain simply opinions - they lack any scriptural sanction. They may be more or less useful (depending on how closely they stick to things that are clearly revealed elsewhere in scripture) but they can never be authoritative. It remains doubtful whether God ever intended each one of these details to have any special meaning.

- The tabernacle cannot be made to teach anything or reveal anything which is not an already established part of the teaching of the NT. The gospel determines the meaning of the tabernacle; the tabernacle does not determine the meaning of the gospel. At all times OT typology must be restricted to illustrating and explaining the doctrines of the NT - the type is merely the "shadow", but the gospel is the substance (Cl 2:17; He 8:5)

The following comments will observe those restraints.

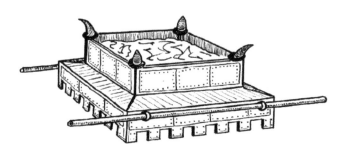

THE CENTRAL MEANING OF THE TABERNACLE

- ## THE PRESENCE OF GOD

  The tabernacle was the place where God manifested his presence -Ex 25:22; 29:42-46; 30:6; Le 16:2; Nu 9:15-16.

- ## ACCORDING TO THE HEAVENLY PATTERN

  Seven times it is stated that the tabernacle was to be made according to God's pattern: Ex 25:9, 40; 26:30; 27:38; Nu 8:4; Ac 7:44; He 8:5.

  This repeated emphasis seems to go beyond the mere requirements of the building itself and shows that God wanted the people to remain vividly aware of the heavenly reality that lay behind the earthly symbol. The tabernacle itself was not reality, but merely represented reality. The old tabernacle was utterly destroyed centuries ago, but its heavenly counterpart remains, and is just as central to our belief and worship as the tabernacle of Moses was to Israel.

What is this heavenly pattern? Some Christian commentators have agreed with the old Jewish rabbis that there is a real tabernacle in heaven, complete with altars, veils, and so on, and that Moses actually saw this heavenly tabernacle while he was on the mountain. He was then instructed to make an exact copy of what he had seen.

While this is not impossible, it seems unlikely, and a more natural understanding of the references given above would take two forms

- God showed Moses a plan, or model, or pattern of what he was to build, and then added the spoken details given in Exodus.

- It was understood that the pattern revealed to Moses represented symbolically heaven itself, and the spiritual principles which control God's relationships with angels and men.

On Ex 25:9 Keil and Delitzsch write -

> . . . a picture of heavenly things or divine realities . . . was shown to Moses that he might copy and embody it in the earthly tabernacle . . . If God showed Moses a picture or model of the tabernacle, and instructed him to make everything exactly according to this pattern, we must assume that in the tabernacle and its furniture heavenly realities were to be expressed in earthly forms; or, to put it more clearly, that the thoughts of God concerning salvation and his kingdom, which the earthly building was to embody and display, were visibly set forth in the pattern shown. The symbolical and typical

significance of the whole building necessarily follows from this, though without our being obliged to imitate the Rabbis, and seek in the tabernacle the counterpart or copy of a heavenly temple. [17]

This fabricating of the tabernacle according to a pattern which accords with heavenly realities justifies our search for the spiritual meaning which underlies the various parts of the tabernacle.

The spiritual value of the tabernacle is further indicated by its association with the number of perfection, "seven". Among other places, this number is found in the seven articles of furniture: the altar of burnt offering, the laver, the table, the lampstand, the altar of incense, the veil, and the ark.

For Israel, the tabernacle was a temporary earthly plan of redemption, based on the perfect heavenly plan; for us, the tabernacle remains a vivid typical picture of the eternal redemption purchased for us by Christ. The central message of the tabernacle, as of the gospel, is Christ.

- **FOR GLORY AND FOR BEAUTY**

The garments of the high priest were made *"for glory and for beauty"* (Ex 28:2, 40). That is, there were two reasons for the instruction to weave these garments out of fine material and in beautiful colours -

  – To glorify God

  – To be beautiful in their own right.

---

[17] Op. cit. pg. 166, 167.

This second reason suggests again that not everything in the tabernacle had a special "meaning". Some of the construction was simply beautiful for its own sake. Then again, other parts were included because they were structurally necessary; or they were made of certain materials simply because these were the best materials available for the required purpose.

- **ATONEMENT**

  The central rite of the tabernacle was celebrated on the annual Day of Atonement, when by the shedding of blood the sins of Israel were covered (Le 16:1, ff.). The high priest could not enter the holy of holies without the shedding and applying of blood (Le 16:2, 11 - 14; He 9:7).

  The Day of Atonement is discussed more fully below, in the chapter on the Feasts of Israel.

  It is through the Day of Atonement that the tabernacle provides its best type of Christ, who brings believers into God's presence by the shedding of his blood. This is clearly explained in Hebrews chapter 9.

  As a research project you could read Hebrews 9 and make notes of the essential similarities, and differences, between atonement in the OT and the atonement of Christ. One important difference is that Jesus is both priest and victim - He presents his own blood.

  This brings me to a fundamental rule for interpreting the tabernacle

    – *because* the OT shows that the central type-value of the tabernacle was to provide access into the presence of God by atonement; and

- *because* the NT shows that the central type-value of the tabernacle is a depiction of the believer entering the presence of God by Christ's atonement;

- *therefore*, every interpretation of the spiritual significance of the tabernacle must be consistent with these two basic concepts;

- *which means*, any interpretation must be rejected that *(i)* teaches that access into the presence of God can be gained by any method other than simple faith in the blood of Christ; *(ii)* denies that every believer is already, and continually, dwelling in the presence of God; *(iii)* separates Christians into diverse groups, some of whom are reckoned to be in the holiest, and some of whom are excluded from the holiest.

Using these principles, the following examples would have to be rejected as wrong interpretations of the tabernacle -

- *Bad example one*: the outer court is salvation; the holy place is water baptism; the holy of holies is Spirit baptism.

- *Bad example two*: the outer court represents the nominal church; the holy place the charismatic churches; and the holy of holies the "true-worshipping" churches.

- *Bad example three*: the three areas represent the kingdom, the body, the bride.

The fault of each of these examples, and of many others like them, is that they divide the people of God into various companies, only some of whom are given access into the true presence of God. But any typology that divides Christians so that some are excluded from the presence of God is false, no matter how logical or appealing it may otherwise seem to be.

SOME POSSIBLE INTERPRETATIONS

Here are *four examples* of valid methods of using the typology of the tabernacle. Many others could be given, but these will help you to distinguish between the *true* and the *false* -

- **THE WAY OF SALVATION**

    See He 9:1, ff., etc.

The Holiest	The Holy	The Laver	The Altar
THE PRESENCE OF GOD	THE BREAD OF LIFE THE INTERCESSION OF CHRIST THE LIGHT OF THE WORLD	THE WORD OF CHRIST	THE CROSS OF CHRIST

KEY: only through Christ can we enter God's presence (He 10:22).

RESEARCH: find scripture references to justify the symbolism indicated for each major part of the tabernacle.

- **THE CHURCH**

    See Ep 2:19-22; 1 Pe 2:4-8.

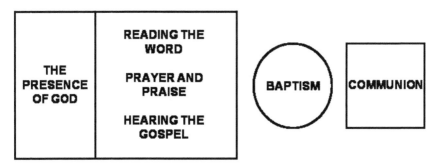

KEY: Baptism, communion, prayer, etc., are all valid parts of worship, but only faith in the sprinkled blood of Christ can usher us into the presence of God.

- **THE BELIEVER**

SPIRIT	SOUL	BODY
THE PRESENCE OF GOD	THE KNOWLEDGE OF GOD	SERVICE FOR GOD

KEY: *Outer Court*: the body <u>sacrificed</u> (*Altar* - Ro 12:1) The body <u>sanctified</u> (*Laver* - 1 Co 6:11)

Holy Place: the soul aware of God through <u>scripture</u> (*Table* and *Lampstand*) and <u>prayer</u> (*Altar of Incense*).

Holy of Holies: the <u>spirit</u> united with God (1 Co 6:17).

Whole Tabernacle: the <u>whole person</u> in fellowship with the lord.

- **HEAVEN AND EARTH**

GOD'S THRONE	HEAVEN LIFE WORSHIP LIGHT	EARTH THE MESSAGE OF SALVATION

KEY: read Re 11:19; 5:1 ff.

SOME MORE DETAILED SYMBOLISM

Here are some suggestions as to how the various parts of the tabernacle can be given a more detailed typological value. The list is by no means exhaustive -

RESEARCH: you would find it instructive to compile your own list first, without consulting the following notes; then you could add to my notes either *(i)* new symbolic meanings; or *(ii)* further details to the meanings given here.

- **GENERAL**

  - The tabernacle was built from free-will offerings

    See Ex 25:1-8; 35:10-29; so much so, that the gifts had to be stopped (36:6-7). See now 1 Co 16:1-2.

  - The people's hearts were stirred to give

    See Ex 35:21. See now 2 Co 9:7-8

  - Special abilities were imparted to the workmen

    See 1 Co 12:28 ff.

All of this symbolises the experience of believers today.

- **THE CLOUD**

    The cloud was

    - a guide (Ex 30:20-22; Nu 9:15-23)

    - a defence (Ex 14:19-25)

    - a presence (Ex 16:10; 33:7-11)

    - a covering (Ex 40:34; Nu 9:15-16; 10:34; Ps 105:39)

    The cloud thus symbolises the Holy Spirit who guides (Ro 8:14), defends (Lu 24:49), and covers (Ps 57:1; 91:1 ff), and who makes real the presence of God (Jn 14:18; 15:26; 16:7; Ps 139:7-12).

    The cloud is also an image of God's eternal protection in his coming Kingdom (Is 4:5-6).

- **THE TABERNACLE STRUCTURE**

    - The external appearance was drab, but the internal appearance was beautiful. So, too, the gospel of Christ appears drab to the unbeliever, but beautiful to the believer (cp. 2 Co 2:14-16).

    - The internal colourings are symbolic -

        white ....purity
        purple.............royalty
        scarlet ....sacrifice
        blue................deity
        gold ....majesty

    These colour associations are a little arbitrary, but they do have scriptural warrant.

    RESEARCH: find appropriate scriptures for the spiritual significance of each colour.

- **THE TABERNACLE MATERIALS**

  Symbolism may be given to at least some of the materials used in the tabernacle; thus -

  - *acacia wood*...the humanity of Christ (Is 53:2)

  - *gold* ....the deity of Christ

  - *silver* ....redemption (Ex 30:11-16; 38:25-27)

  - *fine linen* ....righteousness (Re 19:8)

  - *animal skins*...sacrifice

  - *bronze* ....judgment (Nu 21:6-9)

- **THE COVERINGS**

  - The *embroidered inner covering* (the tabernacle proper) - the glory of Christ, seen only from within the sanctuary.

  - The *goat's-hair tent* - the sin bearer (Le 16:20-22); and perhaps there is a symbolic link with Ca 1:5 (the goat skins were probably black).

  - The *red rams' skins* - the blood of Christ (He 9:22).

  - The *dugong skins* - protection (Ps 27:5).

- **THE OUTER COURT**

  - There was only **one entrance**, facing east, symbolising the one way to God (Jn 14:6; Ma 4:2).

  - The **bronze altar** was the first point of contact after entry. Thus, Christian life begins at the cross (1 Co 1:21-24; 2:1-2; Ga 6:14; and cp. the story in "Pilgrim's Progress").

- The **laver** shows the need for cleansing (He 10:22; Jn 13:3-10). No dimensions are given, so cleansing is unlimited. It was made of bronze mirrors, symbolising the destruction of human pride (Ex 38:8).

- **THE HOLY PLACE**

  - **No chairs** were provided. The priests could never sit down, because their work was never done. But Christ, having finished his work, could take his **seat** in the heavenly sanctuary (He 9:11-14, 23-28; 10:1-4, 11-14).

  - **The table** was made of acacia wood and gold; thus, like the altar of incense and the ark, it symbolises the deity and humanity of Christ. It also provided **nourishment** for the priests; thus Christ having died, been "crushed" and fashioned into the "true Bread", has become the bread of life for his believer-priests (Jn 6: and 12:27-33).

  - **The bread of the presence** symbolises the purpose and plan of God for believers who are "laid out" before him. See Ro 8:28, where the word for "purpose" is the same as that used for the showbread in the LXX version of 1 Sa 21:6.

  - **The lampstand** has the following significance -

    The lamps: Christ, the Light of the World (Jn 8:12).

    The branches: perfection in Christ (cp. Re 4:5).

Pure beaten gold: his sufferings have made Christ immensely valuable to his people (1 Pe 1:17-18; 2:7).

The oil: the Holy Spirit (Is 61:1 ff.).

The light may also symbolise the church (Re 1:20; Mt 5:15-16); and the branches, the nine-fold gifts and nine-fold fruit of the Spirit (1 Co 12:8-11; Ga 5:22-23).

Note that there was no natural light in the tabernacle. Without the lampstand there was darkness (cp. the world without Christ).

– **The altar of incense** has the following significance

The incense: Christ our intercessor (Jn 17:1-26; Ro 8:34; He 7:25); or, the prayers of Christians (Re 8:3-4).

Note that only genuine incense could be used (Ex 30:9-10, 30-38). The significance of this may be discovered in Mt 6:5-8; Ja 1:5-8; Ps 66:18).

- **THE HOLY OF HOLIES**

    – **The veil** represents the person of Christ, particularly his humanity (He 10:19-20; Mt 27:50-51).

    – **The fire** from the altar was taken into the holiest (Le 16:12); thus, Jesus suffered the fire of God's wrath to give us access (Ro 5:1 ff; He 4:14-16; 10:19-25).

    – **The veil** of our flesh still prevents us from gaining full access into the holiest, but we can enter spiritually by faith (He 6:18-20). Hence the altar of incense (which symbolises prayer) stands at the entrance to the holiest.

- **THE ARK OF THE COVENANT OF THE LORD**

The ark was the central feature of the tabernacle (He 9:3-5).

- **The mercy seat** signifies the place from which the mercy of God is freely extended to all who have expressed faith in the sprinkled blood of the sacrifice. The Greek word for *"mercy-seat"* is *"hilasterion"*; it is used in Ro 3:25 where it is translated *"expiation"* (RSV) or *"propitiation"* (AV), that is, *"the satisfying of the righteous demands of God's broken law."*

Note further:

the pure gold indicates that mercy is entirely divine in its source

the crown of gold indicates the divine monarchy

the sprinkling of blood transforms the awesome throne of God into the seat of gentle mercy (Le 16:14)

The cherubim reveal the angels rejoicing in God's wondrous salvation (Lu 15:10) and surrounding the throne of God with reverent praise.

- **The urn of manna** represents the living bread (Jn 6:48) which is eternally available to the true people of God (cp. Ex 16:14-36).

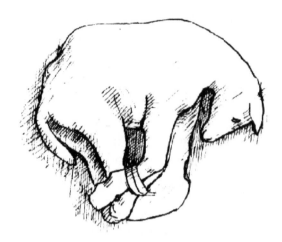

Model of goat trussed up for sacrifice

- **Aaron's rod** (which budded supernaturally) typifies the resurrection to endless life by which Christ as vindicated and established for ever as our High Priest (Ro 1:4; He 7:25; 9:24).

- **The law**, kept inside the ark, represents the righteousness of God which was fully "kept" in Christ (Mt 5:17; Ro 10:4).

  > *Jesus is the Way* (the Law), *the Truth* (the Manna), *and the Life* (the Rod).

- **The cloud**. The presence of the Lord in the cloud which hovered over the ark in the holiest is symbolic of the Holy Spirit; thus, the baptism in the Spirit is available to all who enter beyond the veil, through faith, and by the blood (Jn 1:29, 32-33).

THE SIGNIFICANCE OF THE HIGH PRIEST'S GARMENTS

- **THE EPHOD**

  Its bright colours may be given the same symbolism indicated above.

- **THE ONYX STONES**

  - The engraved names of all the tribes symbolise: remembrance (2 Ti 2:19) and representation (1 Ti 2:15; He 7:25; 1 Jn 2:1).

  - The setting of the stones on the shoulders of the priest symbolise Christ's keeping power (1 Pe 1:5).

- **THE BREAST PIECE**

  Its position over the heart reminds us of the love of Christ; the separate stone for each tribe reminds us that God knows each of his children by name (Is 49:15-16); and the use of twelve different gems reminds us that each believer has his own unique gifts and calling (1 Co 12:4-12).

- **THE URIM AND THUMMIM**

  This signifies the divine guidance which is now available to every believer (Ro 8:14; Jn 16:13).

- **THE ROBE**

  This beautiful blue full-length garment signifies the perfect deity of Christ; the bells around its hem may remind us that just as the ministry of the high priest could not be hidden, so Christ died openly and publicly; and the pomegranates may speak of the sweetness of knowing Christ (Ps 19:7-10; 34:8), and of his surpassing beauty (cp. Ca 4:3).

- **THE TURBAN**

  Its motto, *"Holy to the Lord,"* expresses separation from the world and to God; its theme of purity reminds us that Christ had no blemish (He 4:15); and it was a crown (Ex 29:6; 39:30), thus expressing the royalty of Christ.

- **THE ANOINTING OIL**

  Special anointing oil was used for the consecration of the priests. No imitation was allowed (Ex 30:22-33). So Jesus had a unique anointing (Is 61:1-3); Ac 10:38), and so too have believers (1 Jn 2:26-27). No substitute will do!

CONCLUSION

The tabernacle may be described as an ornate and dynamic picture of the divine plan of redemption. It was a heavenly principle reduced to a human pattern. In it we can see Jesus Christ uplifted and the way of salvation made plain.

An almost endless variety of types can be drawn from the tabernacle and its furnishings and ceremonies. The suggestions given above do not even begin to exhaust this potential, but they do outline some of the most common applications of the tabernacle to the gospel. If this brief study has aroused your curiosity, and you want to study the subject in more detail, you should purchase some of the many books, both popular and serious, on biblical typology, which are currently available.

Now let the apostle close this chapter with his marvellous summary of the message of the tabernacle -

> *Therefore, brethren, since we have confidence to enter the sanctuary by the blood of Jesus, by the new and living way which he opened for us*

through the curtain, that is, through his flesh, and since we have a great priest over the house of God, let us draw near with the true heart in full assurance of faith, with our hearts sprinkled clean from an evil conscience and our bodies washed with pure water. Let us hold fast the confession of our hope without wavering, for he who promised is faithful; and let us consider how to stir up one another to love and good works, not neglecting to meet together, as is the habit of some, but encouraging one another, and all the more as you see the Day drawing near. (He 10:19-25, RSV)

CHAPTER THREE

THE GREAT FEASTS

Each year ancient Israel celebrated three great feasts; **Passover, Pentecost,** and **Tabernacles**. The purpose of this chapter is to examine these feasts, and to show their significance to Israel, to the Church, and to each Christian.

INTRODUCTION

- The sacred number **seven** occurs often in the regulations governing the feasts. The Sabbath day fell on each seventh day of the week. The seventh month of each year was sacred to the Lord. Every seventh year was a year of rest for the whole land. Seven groups of seven years brought the nation to the great year of jubilee which fell on every fiftieth year.

  The feasts of Passover and of Tabernacles began fourteen days (2x7) after the beginning of the month, and both were to be celebrated for seven days. The feast of Pentecost began on the day immediately following a period of forty-nine days (7x7) after the Passover.

  During the full year there were seven days of holy convocation (apart from the weekly Sabbaths).

- Passover, Pentecost, and Tabernacles were all connected with the various stages of the harvest: Passover with the beginning of the harvest, in spring, when the first green ears were cut; Pentecost with the completion of the corn harvest; Tabernacles with the completion of the harvest of fruit, oil, and wine. Thus, at a time of prosperity and abundance, when the people might be most inclined to forget God and to rest content in their own efforts, they were made to remember the Lord and to acknowledge that all their fruitfulness stemmed from his goodness.

It is also worth noting that these feasts were so placed in the year as to cause the least interference with the work of the people: *Passover*, just before the harvest; Pentecost at the end of the harvest, but before the vintage; *Tabernacles* after all the fruits were gathered in.

- These three major festivals commemorated three great events in the history of Israel; namely, the exodus from Egypt, the giving of the law, and the wandering in the wilderness (which was also linked with the conquest of Canaan).

TYPOLOGY

Before going any further, consider again the meaning of "typology" - it is the study of biblical "types", that is, OT persons, events, institutions, or laws, which typify NT truth. Paul refers to them as "shadows" which reflect the reality of Christ (Cl 2:17; He 8:5). Thus, just as a living person casts a shadow before him which indicates his presence, so the OT contains shadows cast by the approaching Christ. Jesus used types on occasion - for example, the Serpent (Jn 3:14-15), Jonah (Mt 12:38-42).

A study of such "shadows" is of great interest; partly for its own sake, but particularly as it leads us ultimately to Christ.

HOW SHOULD TYPES BE IDENTIFIED AND INTERPRETED?

- ## NT TRUTH IS BASIC.

  That is, nothing is to be read into the OT which is not clearly taught in the NT. *"The substance belongs to Christ"* (Cl 2:17).

  This is brought out by the statement in Hebrews that the Mosaic tabernacle was a COPY of heavenly things (He 8:5). Christ's atoning work was not modelled on the tabernacle - rather, the reverse! Hence, any true understanding of the tabernacle involves a clear understanding of Christ. Start with Christ . . . study the tabernacle . . . return (with a clearer under-standing) to Christ –

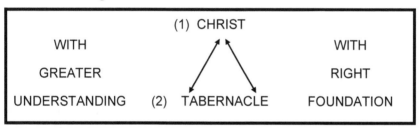

- ## HERMENEUTICS

  Standard principles of interpretation must be applied.

  These involve a consideration

    - of the meaning of words used
    - of background
    - of context and
    - of other scriptures. [18]

---

[18] We recommend for further study on hermeneutics, the following books: by Barry Chant, the author of this present book, "The Secret Is

WHAT WAS THE NATURE OF THE FEASTS?

- ## DIVINELY APPOINTED

  The feasts were divinely appointed (Le 13:1, 2, 44). Hence, they were called

  - the solemn feasts   (Nu 15:3; 2 Ch 8:13)

  - set feasts   Nu 29:39; Ezr 3:5)

  - appointed feasts   (Is 1:14)

  - holy convocations   (Le 23:2, 4, 37)

  Research: Examine the above terms and meditate on their full meaning and significance.

- ## JOYFUL OCCASIONS

  The feasts were called *"cheerful"* (Zc 8:18-19). They were to be kept with joy (Le 23:40; De 16:11, 14-15; Ezr 6:22; Ne. 8:10-12, 17). If any person has thought that religion should be mournful, it is obvious that he is ignorant of the mind of God. It is encouraging to see how the Lord God urged his people to be happy, how few were the times when he required them to weep, and how many the times he urged them to sing. Let your eyes run over the preceding references, let your heart enter into the feel of them, let your imagination take you into each joyful celebration, and let your ear catch the thunderous shouts of praise from the glad multitudes as they danced and sang before the Lord!

Out" (paperback, 128 pages); and by Ken Chant, "Understanding Your Bible" (which is one of the Vision Christian College text books). Both books are available from the College.

- **DIVINE PROTECTION**

  Divine protection was promised to Israel while the menfolk were attending feasts (Ex 14:23-24). No enemy attack would be launched on their land. How fine it would be if our own nation could respond in faith to such a challenge, to seek the kingdom of God and his righteousness above anything else. Then indeed our national safety and prosperity would be guaranteed by God. "Let us check all sinful desires in our own hearts against God and his glory, and then trust him to check all sinful desires in the hearts of others against us and our interest" (Matthew Henry)

- **LARGE GATHERINGS**

  The feasts were to be attended by all the men of Israel (Ex 23:17; 34:23; De 16:16 etc.). However, the whole community was also involved - sons, daughters, servants, visitors etc., (De 16:10-11, 13-14; Ne. 8; Lu 2:41-45). The great festivals of the Lord, and his rich blessing were available to all people without distinction. They were times of sacred convocation, but they were also national gatherings, and there was obviously an atmosphere of holiday festivity surrounding them.

  The Lord Jesus Christ was always careful to be present at the feasts - Mt 26:17-20; Lu 2:41-42; 22:15; Jn 2:13, 23; 5:1; 7-10; 10:22. How arresting to realise that Jesus attended these feasts and no doubt fully entered into a joyful observance of them, even though in many ways they prefigured the dreadful sufferings which were soon to be his.

  Paul attended the feasts whenever he had opportunity to do so (Ac 20:6, 16; 24:11, 17). By doing so he helped to disarm his Jewish foes, and he found opportunity to speak to the crowds about Christ.

WHAT WAS THE SIGNIFICANCE OF THE FEASTS?

The three great feasts each had a threefold significance -

- **HISTORICAL**

    There was a historical significance for Israel; for example, Passover commemorated the deliverance from Egypt; tabernacles the entry into Canaan.

- **PROPHETICAL**

    Each feast also had a prophetical significance: that is, it portrayed in advance some great historical occurrence; so Passover portrayed the passion of Christ; Pentecost portrayed the outpouring of the Spirit.

- **PERSONAL**

    The message of the feasts can be applied personally to the life of the believer: for example, Pentecost, to his baptism in the Spirit; Tabernacles, to his heavenly destiny.

    See further details on this below. See also my Chart of the Feasts at the end of this book.

WHEN WERE THE FEASTS HELD?

- **THE DATES FOR THE FEASTS**

PASSOVER	1st month, 14th day	March - April
PENTECOST	3rd month, 6th day	May - June
TABERNACLES	7th month, 15th day	September - October

- **SPECIAL SABBATHS**

  Note also, that certain days were known as days of holy convocation; that is, as special Sabbath days. There were **seven** of them as follows:

1st month	15th day	First day of Unleavened Bread (that is, of the Passover festival)
	21st day	Last day of Unleavened bread
3rd month	6th day	Day of Pentecost
7th month	1st day	Feast of Trumpets
	10th day	Day of Atonement
	15th day	First day of the Feast of Tabernacles
	22nd day	Last day of the Feast of Tabernacles

  These Sabbaths were in addition to the normal weekly Sabbath.

WHAT WAS THE CENTRAL FEATURE OF THE FEASTS?

The central feature of the feasts was **sacrifice**. Animal sacrifices, grain offerings and burnt offerings were presented according to the pattern set down for each feast. (See Le 23).

WHAT WERE THE BASIC IDEAS BEHIND THE SACRIFICIAL SYSTEM?

- **OFFERING**

  None shall appear before me empty handed (Ex 23:15).

Thus, when approaching God, it was essential to bring a gift of some kind.

Meditation: Consider 2 Sa 24:24.

- **SACRIFICE**

The life of the flesh is in the blood (Le 17:11).

Because of estrangement through sin, men could only approach God when sacrifice for sin had been made.

- **SUBSTITUTION**

A lamb for a household (Ex 12:3).

Not only sacrifice, but substitutionary sacrifice had to be made. The animal suffered as a substitute for the sinner.

Meditation: 1 Co 5:7

WHAT OTHER IDEAS WERE ASSOCIATED WITH SACRIFICES?

- **Holiness** - a lamb without blemish (Le 1:3; etc.)

- **Transference of guilt** - e.g. laying hands on the head of the scapegoat (Le 16:21)

- **Penalty for sin** - the death of the animal (Le 16:11).

- **Personal application** - sprinkling of blood (Le 16:14).

- **Total consecration** - burning of flesh (Le 16:27).

The pattern of the sacrifice of Christ is clearly seen here. This will be brought out in detail below.

Research: Find NT scriptures which relate each of the above points to Christ.

HOW WERE OFFERINGS TO BE PRESENTED?

A detailed description of how the sacrifices were presented is given in Leviticus chapters one to three. You should read these chapters carefully.

Normally, the procedure for animal sacrifices was as follows:

- The offerer brought the animal to the door of the tabernacle, leaned his hand on its head and then slaughtered it on the north side of the altar (Le 1:4, 5, 11; 2, 8; 6:25; 7:2).

- The priest caught the blood in a vessel, and sprinkled some of it on the altar, or the ark etc. (Ex 29:12; Le 4:1).

- The animal was then flayed by the offerer and cut into pieces (Le 1:6; 8:20) and either burnt entirely, or the fat burnt and the remainder burned outside the camp. It was then eaten by the priests or possibly partly by the offerer as well.

- Pigeons were slaughtered, by the priest ringing off the head. The head and body were burned (Le 1:15).

- Vegetable offerings were normally burned and then eaten by the priests. (Le 2:2 ff; 6:9-11; 7:9 ff).

Note the following important points:

- **Fat** was regarded as sacred to the Lord (Le 3:16-17; 7:22-27). It was considered to be the richest part and, therefore, set aside for God (this evidently referred to the suet, not all the fat; see Ne 8:10). "Lest the table of the Lord become contemptible, some things were reserved to it alone" (Matthew Henry).

- **Blood** was also regarded as sacred (Le 7:22-27; 17:11). Blood was synonymous with life, and the sprinkling of the blood signified the substitutionary laying of one's life or soul before God.

WHAT DIFFERENT KINDS OF OFFERINGS WERE THERE?

Sin offerings and guilt offerings were offered *to produce communion* with the Lord. The rest were offered *in recognition that such communion already existed.*

- **SIN OFFERING**

  See Le 4:1-35. Sin offerings were presented for unintentional sins (Le 4:1 ff; Nu 35:9-28), ie. for sins that were not premeditated. They were offered on regular occasions such as the major feasts, or the consecration of priests. They were also offered after sins of ignorance had been committed, and to cleanse leprosy (Le 14:9), women (12:6-8) etc.

  Type of Christ who died to save the sinner from every sin, known and unknown.

- **GUILT OFFERING**

  (Trespass offering - Le 5:1-6:7). Guilt offerings atoned for a particular offence, rather than the person of the offender (Le 5:15 ff). They were offered for failure to honour the Lord, for ignorant transgression of the law (5:17), fraud (6:1), rape (19:20-22), purification of lepers etc., (14:12).

  Type of Christ dying for the injury caused by sin, as well as for its guilt.

- **BURNT OFFERING**

  See Le 1:1-17. Burnt offerings were so named because of the idea of the smoke rising to heaven. They symbolised an entire surrender to God by the individual or congregation. They were offered, not to produce reconciliation, but in recognition of it.

They were offered every morning and evening (Ex 29:38-42); every Sabbath, with double the normal daily offering (Nu 28:9, 10); at the new moon; and at the feasts.

Special burnt offerings were made at the consecration of priests, cleansing of lepers etc. (Le 8:18; 9:12; 14:19). Freewill burnt offerings were also offered (e.g. Nu 7).

Type of Christ offering himself as a sweet savour totally consumed with God's will. They are a type of the believer's consecration, too (Ro 12:1-2).

An Assyrian Winged Genius - the cherubim embroidered on the tabernacle curtains may have resembled these creatures.

- **PEACE OFFERING**

   See Le 3:1-17. Peace Offerings were offered to express communion with God. There were three kinds:

   – thank offering (Le 7:12)

- Votive offering i.e. sacrifice to mark a vow (Le 7:16; Nu 15:3, 8).

- Freewill offering (Le 7:16; 22:18, 21).

They always followed all other sacrifices. They served to make the offender mindful of God when in possession and enjoyment of divine mercies. They maintained a feeling of the presence of God (i.e. not to produce peace, but in recognition of it).

Public peace offerings were made on festive occasions (Ex 24:5; Sa 6:17 etc.), and at the feasts (Nu 10:10). Private offerings could be made (Le 7:16; 22:21 etc.).

Type of Christ our peace (Ep 2:14).

- **CEREAL (MEAL) AND DRINK OFFERINGS**

See Le 2:1-16. Cereal offerings recognised the bounty of God in bestowing earthly blessings, by dedicating to him the best of the gifts - flour, oil, wine (see 1 Ch 29:10-14). They also symbolise spiritual food.

- **Public offerings** were the showbread, the sheaf of wheat at Passover, and the two loaves at Pentecost.

- **Private offerings** were made by the priests (Le 6:14-20) and by poor people (Le 5:11-12) who could not afford sin offerings.

- **Type of Christ** as a man. Unleavened bread, used normally, illustrates his sinless humanity.

- **HEAVE AND WAVE OFFERINGS**

The name comes from the manner of presentation (wave offerings were moved from side to side in the air).

- **Heave offerings** were gifts presented either voluntarily, or by law, for religious purposes; e.g. at the building of a tabernacle (Le 7:14; Ex 25:2 ff; Ezr 8:25 etc.).

- **Wave Offerings** were portions of other offerings - e.g. the breast of a private thank offering (Le 7:30), the first sheaf of Passover (Le 23:20).

Type of gratitude and worship of believers.

- ## RED HEIFER OFFERING

See Nu 19:1ff. This was a special form of sin offering whose ashes were kept to be used in purifying defiled persons (Nu 19:1 ff).

Type of the daily cleansing provided by Christ in the life of the believer.

WHEN WERE OFFERINGS MADE?

- ## DAILY

See Nu 28:3-8.

- Burnt offerings: 1 yearling male lamb without blemish (morning); 1 yearling male lamb without blemish (evening).

- Cereal offering

- Drink offering (wine)

- ## SABBATH

See Nu 28:9-10; Le 24:8).

- Normal daily offerings, plus -

- Burnt offerings: 2 yearling male lambs without blemish.

- Cereal offering.

- Drink offering.

- **NEW MOON**

See Nu 28:11-15.

- Normal daily offerings, plus -

- Burnt offerings: 2 bullocks, one ram, seven yearling male lambs without blemish.

- Cereal offerings in proportion.

- Drink offerings in proportion.

- Sin offering: 1 male goat.

- **PASSOVER**

See Ex 12:1 ff; De 16:1-7. See also notes on Passover (below).

- **UNLEAVENED BREAD**

See Le 23:10-14; Nu 28:16-25. See also notes on Passover.

- **PENTECOST**

See Nu 28:27-31; Le 23:16-20. See also notes on Pentecost.

- **FEAST OF TRUMPETS**

See Nu 29:1-6. See notes on feast of Tabernacles.

- **DAY OF ATONEMENT**

See Le 16:1 ff.

- ## FEAST OF TABERNACLES

See Nu 29:13 ff. See notes on feast of Tabernacles.

References:

For a detailed survey of the sacrificial system you should consult any major Bible Dictionary, or any comprehensive commentary on the OT. The above notes are hardly more than a brief outline. C.W. Slemming provides a good devotional study in his book, "Thus Shalt Thou Serve", Christian Literature Crusade, 1974 (USA edition).

THE THREE MAJOR FEASTS

THE PASSOVER

- ### BIBLICAL BACKGROUND

Read Ex 12:1-49; Ex 23:14-17; Le 23:4-14; Nu 28:16-25; De 16:1-8).

Research: make a list of

- – The events of the first Passover.

- – The procedure for celebrating the feast of Passover each year.

- ### WHAT WAS THE PASSOVER?

The name "Passover" comes from Ex 12:13, where the Lord promised to "pass over" the blood-marked houses of Israelites in Egypt in the days of Moses. The word "Passover" is often taken to mean "passing-by" - that is, the angel of death went straight past the houses of the Israelites and did not harm them. This is certainly a true idea, but it conveys only the negative part of the real thought behind the word. The angel of death **passed by** only because, in fact, the Lord God

passed over the homes of Israel to shield them from hurt. The Saviour defended each house by leaping forward to interpose himself between the house and the angel of death (cp. Is 31:5; De 39:11-12; Ex 12:23).

The Passover feast was kept annually in commemoration of this event.

Because unleaveneq21d bread was sued, the occasion was also called the **feast of unleavened bread**. Technically, the 14th day of the 1st month was called *"Passover"* and the next 7 days *"unleavened bread"* (Le 23:5-6).

The title *"paschal feast"* is sometimes used. This comes from the Greek for *"Passover"* which is *pascha*. Christ is thus called the *"paschal lamb"* (1 Co 5:7, RSV).

- **WHY WAS THE PASSOVER HELD?**

The feast originated in the last of the ten plagues brought upon Egypt through Moses (Ex 12:1 ff). By the last of these, the eldest in every family was slain, unless protective provision was made. The following precautions were necessary (Ex 12:1-13) -

- A year-old lamb or kid without blemish had to be set aside for each household on the 10th day.

- The lamb had to be killed on the evening of the 14th day.

- The blood had to be applied with hyssop to the lintel and doorposts of the house.

- The flesh had to be roasted and eaten that night, with unleavened bread and bitter herbs.

- Anything left over had to be burnt.

     – The people had to be dressed ready for travel.

Each year after this, a similar feast was to be held. Thus, the first Passover feast was held for the saving of the lives of the firstborn of Israel. Successive feasts were in remembrance of this. Josephus talks about the institution of the Passover, and its continued observance in his day -

> But when God had signified, that with one more plague he would compel the Egyptians to let the Hebrews go, he commanded Moses to tell the people that they should have a sacrifice ready, and that they should prepare themselves . . . (When) all were ready to depart, they offered the sacrifice, and purified their houses with the blood, using bunches of hyssop for that purpose; and when they had supped, they burnt the remainder of the flesh, as just ready to depart. Whence it is that we do still offer this sacrifice in like manner to this day, and call this festival "Pascha", which signifies "the feast of the Passover"; because on that day God passed us over, and sent the plague upon the Egyptians; for the destruction of the first-borne came upon the Egyptians that night . . . Accordingly (Pharaoh) called for Moses, and bid them begone, as supposing, that if once the Hebrews were gone out of the country, Egypt should be freed from its miseries. They also honoured the Hebrews with gifts;   some in order to get them to depart quickly, and others

on account of their neighbourhood, and the friendship they had with them. [19]

- **HOW WAS THE PASSOVER OBSERVED?**

  - **DATE**

    Normally, the Passover was celebrated on the 14th day of the 1st month. For reasons of uncleanness or unreadiness on the part of either the people or the priests, the feast could be observed in the second month, on the 14th day (Nu 9:9-12; 2 Ch 30:2-4).

  - **DURATION**

    The feast itself was held on the evening of the 14th day - i.e. running into the beginning of the 15th day (the Hebrew day began at sunset). See Ex 12:6; Le 23:5; cp. Le 23:32. Then followed the seven days of the feast of unleavened bread (15th - 31st). The first and last days were special Sabbaths.

    Note: in the NT. the 14th was called the first day of unleavened bread. See Mt 26:17; Mark. 14:12; Lu 22:7. This was a later development, however. Originally, the day after the Passover, i.e. the 15th, was the first day of unleavened bread. Other innovations had also been introduced by NT times: wine mixed with water was drunk at different stages of the feast (cp. Lu 22:17, 20; Paul called this *"the cup of blessing"*, 1 Co 10:16); Psalms were sung, notably the *"Hallel"* (Ps 113-Ps 118: see Mt 26:30; Mk 14:26); and the Passover meal was

---

[19] Op. cit., Bk. 2, 14, 6.

not eaten standing (as it had been in Egypt), but reclining (as at the Last Supper).

– SACRIFICES

In addition to the daily offerings, which continued as usual, the following sacrifices were made:

PASSOVER 14th day Ex 12:1 ff., De 16:1-7	• Passover lamb • bitter herbs • unleavened bread	

| _UNLEAVENED BREAD_ 15th to 21st days Nu 28:16-25 | • burnt offerings | 2 bullocks 1 ram without blemish 7 male yearling lambs without blemish |
| | • cereal offering • sin offering • drink offering | 1 male goat wine |

No leavened bread to be eaten at any time during this festival (Ex 12:14-20; De 16:3-4)

| _FIRST FRUITS_ 16th day Le 23:10-14 | • barley sheaf as a wave offering • burnt offering | 1 male yearling lamb without blemish |
| | • cereal offering • drink offering | wine |

– SOLEMNITY

Initially, anyone who failed to keep the feast, or who failed to keep it properly, was to be cut off from the people (Ex 12:19; Nu 9:13).

Only Israelites were to take part. No foreigner was permitted (Ex 12:43-45). However, proselytes were able to participate (Ex 12:44; Nu 9:14).

Thus, the importance of the Passover was stressed.

This is how Josephus describes its observance -

. . . the law ordained that we should every year slay that sacrifice which I before told you we slew when we came out of Egypt, and which was called the "Passover"; and so do we celebrate this "Passover" in companies, leaving nothing of what we sacrifice till the day following. The feast of unleavened bread succeeds that of the PPassover, and falls on the fifteenth day of the month, and continues seven days, wherein they feed on unleavened bread; on every one of which days two bulls are killed and one ram, and seven lambs. Now these lambs are entirely burnt, beside the kid of the goats which is added to all the rest, for sins; for it is intended as a feast for the priest on every one of those days. But on the second day of unleavened bread, which is the sixteenth day of the month, they first partake of the fruits of the earth, for before that day they do not touch them. And while they suppose it proper to honour God, from whom they obtain this plentiful provision, in the first place, they offer the first-fruits of their barley, and that in the manner following: They take a handful of the ears, and dry them, then beat them small, and purge the barley from the bran; they then bring one tenth deal to the altar, to God: and, casting one handful of it upon the fire, they leave the rest for the use of the priest; and after this it is that they may publicly or privately reap their harvest. 20

- **HOW OFTEN WAS THE PASSOVER OBSERVED?**

The feast was intended to be kept annually, of course. The following celebrations of the Passover are recorded in scripture.

- At the Exodus (Ex 12:28; Nu 33:3-4

- One year later (Nu 9:1-5)

- Soon after entering Canaan (Ex 13:5; Js 5:10)

- During the period of the Judges (2 Kg 23:22-23)

- In Samuel's day (2 Ch 35:18)

- Under King Solomon (2 Ch 8:12-13)

- Under King Hezekiah (2 Ch 30:1-27)

- Under King Josiah (2 Ch 35:1-19)

- After the exile (Ezr 6:19-22)

---

[20] Ibid. Bk. 3,10,5. Elsewhere Josephus states that in his day the priests slew the Passover lambs "from the ninth hour to the eleventh", and that not less than ten people were represented by each lamb. He tells of a time when the number of lambs slain at a particular Passover was 256,500.

– In Jesus; day (Mt 26:1 ff; Mk 14:1 ff; Lu 2:41 ff; 21:1 ff; Jn 2:13 ff; 6:4; 11:55 ff; 18:28; 19:14)

There are a number of other references to *"annual feasts"* (e.g. 1 Ch 23:31; 2 Ch 2:4; 8:13; Ezr 3:5; Ne 10:33; La 1:4; 2:6-7; Ezr 45:17 ff; 46:9-11; etc. Note 2 Ch 8:13)

- **WHAT WAS THE SIGNIFICANCE OF THE PASSOVER?**

This question is answered quite specifically in Ex 12:26-27 -

> *And when your children say to you "What do you mean by this service?" you shall say, "It is the sacrifice of the Lord's Passover, for he passed over the houses of the people of Israel in Egypt, when he slew the Egyptians but spared our houses." And the People bowed their heads and worshipped.*

Thus, the feast was a perpetual reminder of the deliverance of Israel from Egypt.

There are further aspects of this:

– **SUBSTITUTION**

The lamb was a substitute for the firstborn in each household - thus averting the judgment of God (Ex 12:12-13)

– **UNLEAVENED BREAD**

Unleavened bread was a sign of the affliction suffered by Israel in Egypt and of the haste with which they left. Hence, it is called *"the bread of affliction"* (De 16:3)

– **FIRST FRUITS**

This was a sign of gratitude to God for the safe arrival of Israel in Canaan; which, of course, was the climax of the exodus begun in Egypt (Le 23:10-11). Furthermore, the Passover, like the other two great feasts, was thus connected with the agricultural year.

(**Note**: Although not specifically stated, the First fruits would have been of the barley harvest, which came in April-May. The wheat ripened about 3 weeks later.)

The Passover was in effect the New Year celebration of Israel. With this feast their year began. By it they were taught that all life, deliverance, and prosperity has its beginning in God. They were taught to humbly depend upon God for his goodness in the coming year. In this feast they remembered that once they had been slaves, and that if God failed to protect them they would soon be slaves again.

• **WHAT IS THE SIGNIFICANCE OF THE PASSOVER FOR CHRISTIANS?**

The Passover is far more significant for Christians than it now is to the Jews, who still see the feast as essentially of historical - agricultural significance. Christians see in it an explicit and challenging type of Christ.

RESEARCH:

Before reading on, examine the key scriptures given at the beginning of these notes on the Passover and make a list of their typological value.

– THE LAMB (EX 12:1-12).

Clearly a type of Christ (Jn 1:29).

Note the following:

A male in its prime (vs. 5)

So Jesus was cut off in the prime of manhood (cp. Ps 102:23, 24).

Without blemish (vs. 5)

So Jesus was without sin (He 7:26-27; 1 Pe 1:18-19)

Killed as a substitute (vs. 1-12).

So Jesus died in our place (Ro 5:6 etc.).

Roasted whole (vs. 8-10).

So Jesus suffered completely for our sins, giving himself totally (cp. the Gethsemane prayer). In later times it became customary to fix the lamb on two pieces of wood placed across each other, thus making an unwitting type of Calvary.

With unleavened bread and bitter herbs (vs. 8).

Calvary was not pleasant (Mt 26:38 ff; 27:45-46).

– THE BLOOD (EX 12:7-23).

Essential for deliverance (vs. 13, 23).

So the blood of Christ is essential for our deliverance (Ep 1:7; He 9:22).

Applied to the door posts etc. (vs. 7).

It was not sufficient for the blood to be shed; it also had to be sprinkled, using a basin and hyssop. So the blood of Christ has been shed, but it will do us no good unless we pick up the basin of the covenant, and with the hyssop of faith apply to ourselves the benefit of his sacrifice (1 Pe 1:2; He 10:22).

A sign of God (vs. 13).

So the blood of Jesus identifies God's people today (1 Pe 1:2; Ac 20:28).

Protection from judgment (vs. 8, 10).

So the blood of Jesus averts the wrath of God (He 10:19; 1 Jn 1:7; Ro 5:9)

– **THE MEAL (EX 12:8-49).**

The whole lamb to be eaten (vs. 8, 20).

So we must wholeheartedly partake of Christ and be completely devoted to him (Mt 20:20-28; Jn 6:53-56).

Unleavened bread and bitter herbs (v8).

So there must be no sin in the life of the believer (1 Co 5:6-8) although the experience of repentance and cleansing may be bitter (2 Co 7:9-10). The bitter herbs may also suggest a prophecy of the bitterness which will grip the people of Israel in time to come when they see Christ appear in his glory and realise that they slew their own Messiah, just as they had by their own hands slain the lamb-cp. Zc 12:10, which speaks of this day of bitterness for Israel, and also alludes to the death of the first-born in Egypt, the death of the firstborn lambs, and the bitter herbs the people ate on that first Passover night.

Eaten in haste (vs. 11).

So the believer has no permanent dwelling place on earth - he is but a pilgrim (1 Pe 2:11).

Strength for the journey (vs. 11,31ff).

So Christ nourishes the believer day by day (2 Co 4:7-16).

None left till morning (vs. 10).

Christ must be received now (cp. 2 Co 6:1-2).

Only for Israelites (vs. 43-49).

So only the redeemed people of God may share in the kingdom (Mt 22:11-14).

– UNLEAVENED BREAD (EX 12:14 FF).

Made without leaven (vs. 15).

The bread used in the Passover celebrations had to be unleavened (see also De 16:3). It was called *"the bread of affliction"*, because by it Israel was reminded of their past suffering as loaves. Before eating the rich, yeasted bread made from the new wheat, they were to eat this sorrowful bread, and remember with humility the deliverance God had wrought for them.

Leaven was also forbidden in the cereal offerings (Le 2:11; 6:17); during the ordination of a priest (Ex 29:2, 23); among Nazarite offerings (Nu 6:15); and in the showbread -

> . . . baked bread was set on the table
> of shewbread, **without leaven**, of
> twenty-four tenth deals of flour . . .

two heaps of these were baked; they were baked the day before the Sabbath, but were brought into the holy place on the morning of the Sabbath, and set upon the holy table, six on a heap, one loaf still standing over-against another; where two golden cups full of frankincense were also set upon them, and there they remained until another sabbath, and then other loaves were brought in their stead, while the loaves were given to the priests for their food . . . [21]

As the bread has no leaven, so our Lord Jesus Christ had no corruption (2 Co 5:21; He 4:15). So, too, we are warned against the *"leaven"* of the Pharisees and Sadducees (Mt 16:1-12); of Herod (Mk 8:15); of legalism (Ga 5:9); of carnality, and against the way that sin affects the whole person (as leaven does the whole loaf - 1 Co 5:6).

MEDITATION:

Consider the different "brands" of leaven in each of the above cases. What differences are there?

Made with salt (cp. Le 2:13).

So Jesus is indestructible (He 7:16) and pure (He 7:26). Similarly, the believer is joined to the Lord by an everlasting covenant (cp. Nu 18:19; 2 Ch 13:5); and is to be a purifying agent

---

[21] Josephus, op. cit., Bk. 3,10,7.

in the earth (Mt 5:13; Mk 9:49-50; Lu 14:34, cp. Cl 4:6).

No leaven in the house (vs. 15-19).

So believers are to be ruthless in searching out every sin (1 Co 5:6-8); Ga 5:2-15; note vs. 9).

Offenders to be cut off (vs. 9).

So it is a serious matter to partake of the Lord's blessings (cp. 1 Co 10:14-22).

For seven days (vs. 15, 19, 20).

The number 7 indicates perfection - so after the salvation of the Passover comes the perfecting of unleavened bread (cp. Mt 5:48; Ep 4:11 ff; He 6:1)

– **FIRST FRUITS (LE 23:10-14).**

The first of the harvest (vs. 10).

The very first grain was presented to God (De 16:9). So we seek first God's kingdom (Mt 6:33).

Presented to the priest (vs. 10).

So the believer's first and best must be offered to God, through Christ (cp. He 13:15 - *"through him. . . "*).

Basis of acceptance (vs. 11).

So when Christ presents the believer's giving of his best to the Lord, he finds acceptance (Ro 12:1; Ep 1:6, A.V.).

Accompanied by burnt offering (vs. 12).

So total commitment of the believer is essential (Ro 12:1-2).

Kept in the Promised Land (vs. 12).

First fruits could not be offered until after entry into Canaan. Thus they signify new life. So Christ is our first-fruits. (1 Co 15:20-23), being the first to rise from the dead.

The day after the Sabbath (vs. 11).

So Christ was raised on the first day of the week (Mk 16:1 etc.). Note, however: the *"Sabbath"* in Le 23:11 was, in fact, probably the first day of unleavened bread, and may not have been the weekly Sabbath.

A wave offering (vs. 11).

So Christ was lifted up before God in his resurrection and ascension.

– **SACRIFICES (NU 28:16-25).**

Burnt offerings (vs. 19).

Again, total commitment (Ro 12:1-2 etc.).

Cereal and drink offerings (vs. 20-24).

So the believer offers his goods and possessions to God (Ac 5:32; 1 Co 16:2)

Sin offering (vs. 22).

So Jesus is the sin offering for the believer (He 7:27).

– **HOLY CONVOCATIONS (NU 28:18-25).**

So the believer can rest in Christ from all *"laborious work"* (Hebrews 4).

– **FELLOWSHIP**

When Israel observed the Passover the nation was united with God and within itself. Family groups came together in love to eat the paschal lamb; and then on the day of convocation that followed, vast multitudes thronged together around the sanctuary. They shared deep and happy fellowship; they united in joyful worship.

The ground for this happiness was the grace of God and the blood of the sacrifice -for by his own choosing and favour the Lord had brought them out of Egypt with a mighty arm, and had covered their sin with the innocent blood of the lamb.

As we celebrate our paschal feast, the Eucharist, we too are reminded to *"discern the body of Christ"*, that is, to recognise that we all make up one Body bound together in Christ our head. **Healing** came to Israel of old as they ate that first paschal meal with true and reverend hearts (cp. Ps 105:37, A.V.). The apostle warns that **sickness** may come to us if we fail to do the same! (1 Co 11:29-30).

Christ: Paul summarises the whole Passover type in four sentences -

> *Do you not know that a little leaven leavens the whole lump? Cleanse out the old leaven that you may be a new lump, as you really are unleavened. For Christ, our paschal lamb, has been sacrificed. Let us, therefore, celebrate the festival, not with the old leaven, the leaven of malice and evil, but with the unleavened bread of sincerity and truth (1 Co 5:6-8).*

- **HOW IS THE PASSOVER OBSERVED TODAY?**

The Jews of today continue to celebrate the passover largely as in the days of the second temple. Several days before the festival all utensils are cleansed; on the eve of the 13th. Nisan the master of the house, with a candle or lamp, searches most diligently into every hole and crevice of the house to discover any leaven which may remain about the premises. Before doing so he pronounces the benediction, following with the formal renunciation of all leaven.

On the 14th. Nisan (the Preparation Day) all the first-born males above thirteen years of age fast, in commemoration of the sparing of the Jewish firstborn in Egypt. On this evening the Jews arrayed in festive garments, offer up the appointed prayers in the synagogue. Returning to their homes they find them illuminated and the tables spread with the following food: Three unleavened cakes are put on a plate; a shank bone of a shoulder of lamb, having a small bit of meat thereon, and an egg roasted hard in hot ashes, are in another dish; the bitter herbs are in a third dish, while the sauce (He "*charoseth*") and salt water, or vinegar, are put into two cups.

The whole family, including the servants, are gathered around the table, and the food, with four cups of wine, is partaken of with blessings and benedictions. The same service is gone through the following evening, as the Jews have doubled the days of holy convocation. [22]

PENTECOST

- **BIBLICAL BACKGROUND**

Read Ex 23:14-17; Le 23:4-14; Nu 28:16-25; De 16:1-8.

---

[22] M. Unger: Bible Dictionary, Moody Press, 1957, p. 356.

Research:

Read the above scriptures and make a list of the most important aspects of the feast of Pentecost.

- **WHAT WAS THE FEAST OF PENTECOST?**

The name *"Pentecost"* is not used in the O.T. at all. It occurs only three times in the N.T. (Ac 2:1; 20:16; 1 Co 16:8).

It is derived from the Greek adjective *pentekostos* which means *"fiftieth"*. Thus it refers to the feast that was held on the fiftieth day after the first day of the feast of unleavened bread.

In the O.T. this festival is given three names . . .

- **THE FEAST OF HARVEST (EX 23:16).**

    The feast usually fell in May-June, i.e. at harvest time.

- **THE FEAST OF WEEKS (LE 23:`15 FF).**

    It occurred seven weeks (that is a **week** of weeks) after the feast of unleavened bread. Although the instructions are somewhat indefinite, it seems that the date was calculated thus:

    Begin with the second day of unleavened bread, that is, the day on which the sheaf of First fruits was waved before the Lord (Le 23:10-11).

    This is the *"morrow after the Sabbath"* (vs. 15); that is, not the weekly Sabbath, but the *"holy convocation"* (which was the 15th. Nisan, the first day of unleavened bread).

    Add seven weeks to this, plus one day, making fifty in all (vs. 15-16).

- **THE DAY OF FIRST FRUITS (NU 28:26).**

  At Pentecost, an offering of two loaves, the first from the new harvest, was presented. This was called *"First-fruits"* (Le 23:17). (This is not to be confused with the first-fruits of a sheaf of barley offered at the feast of unleavened bread).

  The feast was thus a harvest festival, held for one day, just over seven weeks after the Passover. Because of this, it could not be fully celebrated until Israel entered the Promised Land (Le 23:10; 22 etc.).

- **WHY WAS THE FEAST HELD**

  - **HARVEST CELEBRATION**

    Hence the First fruits offering.

  - **THANKSGIVING**

    Thanksgiving was expressed by the bringing of free-will offerings to the Lord (De 16:10).

  - **THE LAW**

    It is thought that the Law of Moses may have been given at Sinai at the time of Pentecost. (Compare Ex 12:1-2 with Ex 19:1).

- **HOW WAS PENTECOST OBSERVED?**

  - **DATE**

    50 days after the first day of unleavened bread; that is, usually the 5th. 6th or 7th of Sivan (May-June).

  - **DURATION**

    The festival was for one day only.

– SACRIFICES AND OFFERINGS

The distinctive offering was *"two loaves of bread to be waved, made of two tenths of an ephah . . . of fine flour . . . baked with leaven"* (Le 23:17). The use of leavened bread was unusual (see above on the feast of unleavened bread). Leavened bread was, however, allowed as part of a peace offering (Le 7:11-14) as well as here at Pentecost. But in these cases it was **never to be burned on the altar** (as cereal offerings normally were, at least in part - Le 2:9). It was to go direct to the priest (Le 2:11-12; 23:20).

Leavened bread was that which was normally used by the people. Therefore this offering indicates the simple giving of the product of their everyday lives to God.

Further offerings were made as follows (Le 23:15-21; Nu 28:26 ff) -

The normal daily offerings, plus

- ◆ *Wave offering*
  2 leavened loaves as First fruits

- ◆ *Burnt offerings*
  7 male yearling lambs without blemish; 1 bullock without blemish; 2 rams without blemish

- ◆ *Cereal offering*
  as for new moon

- ◆ *Drink offering*
  as for new moon

◆ *Sin offering*
1 male goat without blemish

◆ *Peace offering*
2 male yearling lambs without blemish (for the priest) (or wave offering)

– HOLY CONVOCATION

The day of Pentecost was a *"holy convocation"* on which there was to be *"no laborious work"*. People were to gather together for the occasion (*"convocation"* = *"calling together"*) In NT days, Jews came from all over the known world for the celebration (Ac 2:5-11; 20:16).

– REJOICING

The day was one of rejoicing (De 16:9-12). Indeed, the people were commanded to rejoice!

• HOW OFTEN WAS THE FEAST OF PENTECOST OBSERVED?

It was intended to be kept annually, of course. A number of OT references speak of the **three annual feasts** (see 2 Ch 8:13. See above on *"Passover"*).

Otherwise, there are no specific records of the feast being kept in the OT. Only Ac 2 in the NT gives any details of specific examples of the keeping of Pentecost. That the feast was kept is, however, indicated by Ac 20:16 and 1 Co 16:8.

Josephus describes Pentecost and its observance:

When a week of weeks has passed over after this sacrifice (which weeks contain forty and nine days), on the fiftieth day, which is Pentecost . . . they bring to God a loaf, made of wheat flour, of two tenth deals, with leaven; and for sacrifices, they bring two lambs; and when they have only presented them to God, they are made ready for supper for the priests; nor is it permitted to leave anything of them until the day following. They also slay three bullocks for a burnt offering, and two rams; and fourteen lambs, with two kids of the goats, for sins; nor is there any one of the festivals but in it they offer burnt offerings; they also allow themselves to rest on every one of them. Accordingly the law prescribes in them all what kinds they are to sacrifice, and how they are to rest entirely, and must slay sacrifices in order to feast upon them . . . nor is it lawful for us to journey, either on the Sabbath-day, or on a festival day. [23]

- ## WHAT IS THE SIGNIFICANCE OF THE FEAST OF PENTECOST FOR CHRISTIANS?

  - ### HARVEST (EX 23:16).

    The fields are white to harvest (Jn 4:35). Pentecost challenges the believer to see the harvest brought in (cp. Lewi Pethrus: "Pentecost was not given for the church, but for the world"). Hence the need for the power of the Holy Spirit. The present-day move of the Spirit may well be seen as the *"latter-rain"* of James 5:7-8.

  - ### FIRST FRUITS (LE 23:17).

    The leavened loaves represent the first results of the harvest. This may signify a number of things. . .

---

[23] Ibid. Bk. 3, 10, 6; Bk. 13, 8, 4.

Arrival in the Promised Land (cp. Ep 2:19).

The freewill offering of our talents, abilities, fruit etc. to God (De 16:10; 1 Co 6:19-20 etc.). The leavened loaves signify our ordinary, everyday products being offered to God.

The fruitfulness of the Spirit-filled life (Ga. 5:21-22).

The believer, who is fashioned by God into his shape, thus being his *"creatures"* (Ja 1:18). The leaven indicates that while sin has been forgiven, the believer is not yet fully purged from it - he still awaits that day (Ro 8:19-23; 1 Pe 1:5).

Fellowship and unity. Just as the grain is ground into flour, mixed with oil and yeast, kneaded and baked, so believers are broken, brought into fellowship, purified by fire (Mt 3:11) and united into one loaf.

The Holy Spirit himself, who is the guarantee of our inheritance (Ep 1:13) the First fruits of a much greater bounty to come (Ro 8:23).

The leavened loaves are not burned on the altar. Thus, unlike Christ, the Holy Spirit is not offered as a sacrifice for sins. He simply comes to the believer-priest to nourish and sustain him.

Thus, the day of Pentecost in Acts 2 was the giving of the First fruits to the church in glorious anticipation of what was still to come (He 6:5).

Furthermore, it is by the Holy Spirit that the *"leaven"* of the Kingdom of God is spread throughout the world (Mt 13:33).

(Note that leaven here does not indicate corruption, as it usually does. Here, it symbolises a good influence; cp. the serpent, which normally indicates the devil, but in John 3:14 is used of Christ. The lion is also used as a type of both Satan and Christ).

– SACRIFICES

The offerings of animals stress the continuous and unchanging need for cleansing through the blood of Christ (sin offerings), total conse-cration (burnt offerings), and thanksgiving (peace offerings), all presented to God. (See above on sacrifices.)

– HOLY CONVOCATION

The outpouring of the Holy Spirit continues to bring people together from all over the world to find rest in Christ; (cp. Is 28:12).

– REJOICING

De 16 forms a pattern for Christian worship. Believers should still worship with joy, especially when filled with the Holy Spirit (Ac 2:46).

MEDITATION:

Is there a conflict between calling a feast a *"solemn"* occasion (Le 23:3, 21) and yet commanding that it be a time of rejoicing?

Relate this to church worship today.

Can you be commanded to rejoice?

- **THE NAME OF THE LORD**

  The celebration of the feast was permissible only at the place of the Lord's choosing, to make his name dwell there (De 16:11). Jerusalem was eventually accepted as the place where God's name dwelt - 1 Kg 14:21.

- **THE LAW**

  Contrast what happened at Sinai (Ex 19:16 ff) with what happened in the upper room (Ac 2:1-4).

  Both were attended by supernatural signs of God's power and presence. But the law of Spirit and life is rather different from the law of sin and death (Ro 8:2; see also Jn 1:17).

- **CONCLUSION**

  God warned Israel to be careful to observe these statutes, and to remember that they had been slaves in Egypt (De 16:12).

  Better to keep the Lord's commands - even if they are difficult - than to return to slavery! Living the Spirit-filled life may not be easy, but it is certainly better than the alternative!

TABERNACLES

- **BIBLICAL BACKGROUND**

  Read Ex 23:14-17; 34:22-24; Le 16:1-34; 23:23,44; Nu 29:1-40; De 16:13-17.

  RESEARCH:

  On the basis of the above scriptures, make a list of the basic features of . . .

The feast of trumpets.

The Day of Atonement.

The feast of tabernacles.

- **WHAT WAS THE FEAST OF TABERNACLES?**

The Feast of Tabernacles is known in scripture as . . .

- **THE FEAST OF BOOTHS**

(That is, tabernacles.) See Le 23:34; 2 Ch 8:13; Ezr 3:4; Zc 14:16-19; Jn 7:2.

This title perhaps finds its origin in Ex 12:37 (*succoth* is the Hebrew word for booths). It refers to the construction of booths, which was the central rite of the feast.

The word *"tabernacle"* actually means *"tent"* (see Tabernacle notes). Beware of confusing the study of the Tabernacle of Moses with the study of the Feast of Tabernacles.

- **FEAST OF INGATHERING**

See Ex 23:16; Le 2:39; De 16:13.

The feast occurred in autumn after the harvest had been gathered in. It was thus a feast of rest and rejoicing.

- **FEAST OF THE LORD**

See Le 23:39.

All feasts could claim this title, no doubt. But this feast is specially identified in this way.

- **THE FEAST OF THE SEVENTH MONTH**

See 1 Kg 8:2; 2 Ch 5:3.

The reasons for this title are obvious.

- ## WHY WAS THE FEAST OF TABERNACLES OBSERVED?

There were three basic parts to the feast. These were:

- ### THE FEAST OF TRUMPETS

  See Le 23:23-35. Held on the first day of the 7th month.

  Purpose: To announce the beginning of the seventh month - a Sabbath month, which was the sacred month of the year (cp. the trumpet blast which proclaimed the holy year of jubilee, after *"seven weeks of years"* - Le 25:8-12).

  It was the act by which "the congregation presented the memorial of itself loudly and strongly before Jehovah . . . that he might bestow on them the promised blessings of his grace . . . his covenant" (Keil-Delitzsch. pg. 445 on Le 23:23-25).

  The calendar of ancient Israel embraced two separate years: the sacred year, and the civil year. The sacred year began with Passover in the month of Abid (March-April). The civil year began six months later, in the seventh month of the sacred year. It was in this month that the Feast of Trumpets, the Day of Atonement, and the Feast of Tabernacles took place. The first three weeks of the seventh month were occupied with these combined celebrations. This was the final great festive season in the religious year of ancient Israel, and it was also the season which ushered in their "new year's day", the beginning of their civil year.

Our calendar is solar; that is, it is based on the movement of the sun. Israel's calendar was lunar; that is, it was based on the movement of the moon. Their months began with the rising of the new moon, and were each ushered in by the sound of trumpets. But the first day of the seventh month was given special honour. For this day - the start of another year, the preface to atonement, the beginning of tabernacles - the trumpets were blown as they were on no other day!

– THE DAY OF ATONEMENT

See Le 23:26-32.

Purpose: to make atonement (that is, covering) for the sins of Israel, so that they could all *"be clean before the Lord"* (Le 16:30).

Although known sins could be dealt with during the year through regular sin offerings, many sins would not be covered. The Day of Atonement provided a perfect and complete cleansing for all sins (Le 16:30).

Furthermore, the tabernacle was also fully cleansed from defilement on this day (16:33).

– THE FEAST OF BOOTHS

See Le 23:33-36, 39-43. Held on the 15th until the 22nd day and 7th month.

Purpose: to remind the people of God's protection during their journey in the wilderness (Le 23:43). In scripture, a booth signifies protection (Ps 27:5; 91:1, 9; Is 4:5-6).

- **HOW WAS THE FEAST OF TABERNACLES OBSERVED?**

To examine this it will be necessary to study each part in detail:

- **THE FEAST OF TRUMPETS**

See Le 23:23-25.

The trumpet used here was the *shophar*, a large horn which produced a dull, far-reaching tone.

The blast of the *shophar* was additional to the normal blowing of silver trumpets on the first of each month (Nu 10:10). It distinguished the seventh month.

It is often assumed that the details given in Nu 10 for the use of the silver trumpets applied to the feast of trumpets. However, the silver trumpet was different from the *shophar* - it was probably long and straight (not curved) and gave a more high-pitched note. According to Nu 10, the silver trumpets were blown -

To summon the congregation (Nu 10:1-3).

To summon the leaders of the congregation (vs. 4).

To announce the breaking of camp (vs. 5-6).

To call to battle (vs. 9).

To draw attention to burnt offerings and peace offerings at the feasts and new moons (that is, the first of the month vs. 10).

A summary of OT references to both kinds of trumpet shows that, apart from these specific uses, the silver trumpet tended to be used at times of rejoicing while the shophar was used more at times of war and judgment.

The trumpets signified a day of happy gathering! A day of pleasant rest! A day of loud and gleeful celebration as the trumpets sounded in gladness for the New Year! And a day of special sacrifices, *"burnt offerings for a sweet savour,"* showing the gratitude of the people to God, and their willing consecration of themselves to the Lord.

Not that it was always kept this way. The people obeyed the law of suspension of all work on the day of the feast, but they often fell short of putting its meaning into practice in their daily lives - see Am 8:4-6. Tradition has it that the Levites sung the words of Ps 81 on this joyful day of trumpets, and the first three verses of this psalm describe the great gladness which was to characterise the keeping of the feast; also Ps 89:15, *"Blessed are the people who know the festal shout, who walk, O Lord, in the light of thy countenance."*

The use of trumpets in ancient Israel is detailed in the chart on the following page.

A very different application of the sound of the trumpets was made by C.H. Spurgeon, when he urged young preachers -

> Serve God with such education as you have, and thank him for blowing through you if you are a ram's horn; but if there be a possibility of your becoming a silver trumpet, choose it rather."
>
> *(Lectures to My Students, 1970 ed., p. 207).*

Let the music sound forth melodiously from the silver trumpets, as truth rides through the streets.

(Ibid., p. 133).

You are not singers, but preachers... A trumpet need not be made of silver, a ram's horn will suffice: but it must be able to endure rough usage, for trumpets are for wars' conflicts, not for the drawing-room of fashion.

(Ibid., p.110).

THE USE OF TRUMPETS IN THE OT

SILVER TRUMPET

Specific uses	- Nu 10:1-10; 2 Kg 12:13; 2 Ch 29:26-28.
Rejoicing	- 2 Kg 11:14.
Return of ark	- 1 Ch 13:8, 15:24, 28; 16:6, 42.
Music, praise	- 2 Ch 5:12-13; 20:28; 23:13; Ps 98:6.
Rebuilding of Temple	- Ezr 3:10; Ne 12:35-41.
Battle alarm	- 2 Ch 13:12-14; Ho 5:8.

SHOPHAR

Specific uses	- Le 23:23-25; 25:9.
Sinai	- Ex 19:16 ff; 20:18.
Fall of Jericho	- Js 6:4-20.
Gideon	- Jg. 6:34; 7:8 ff.
Return of ark	- 2 Sa 6:15.
Anointing of the King	- 1 Kg 1:34-41; 2 Kg 9:13.
Various battles Insurrections (etc.)	- Jg 3:27; 1 Sa 13:3; 2 Sa 2:28; 15:10; 18:16; 20:1, 22; Ne 4:18-20; Jb 39:24-25; Ps 47:5; Je 4:5; 4:19-21; 6:1, 17; 42:14; 51:27; Ez 33:3-6.
Judgment	- Is 18:3; 58:1; Ho 8:1; Jl 2:1, 15; Am 2:2; 3:6; Zp 1:16; Zc 9:14

Sacrifices were also offered on this day in addition to the normal new moon offerings. These were burnt offerings of 1 bullock, 1 ram and 7 yearling lambs, with cereal and drink offerings in proportion (Nu 29:1-6).

– **THE DAY OF ATONEMENT** (Le 23:26-32; 16:1 ff).

The Day of Atonement was the most solemn and important day in the Hebrew calendar. It was the only feast day on which all work was forbidden (Le 23:26-31).

On this day, all the people were to *"afflict themselves"*, that is, to humble and deny themselves. It is usually thought that this included fasting (cp. Ps 35:13 - hence also the specific instructions in Le 23:32 *"from evening to evening"*). If this is so, then this was the only time of fasting specifically prescribed in the Mosaic Law. For this reason the Day of Atonement came to be often referred to as *"The Fast"* (cp. Ac 27:9; Josephus, **Antiquities**, 14, 16, 4.).

A detailed description of the procedure for the Day of Atonement is given in Leviticus 16. This may be summarised as follows (note that some details are mentioned more than once in Le 16):

Preparations

Aaron had to:

> Provide a young bullock for a sin offering and a ram for a burnt offering.
>
> Bathe his body in water.
>
> Put on plain linen garments.
>
> Take from the congregation two male goats for a sin offering and one ram for a burnt offering.

Cast lots upon the goats: one for the sin offering, and one as a scapegoat (lit. *"for Azazel"*; see below).

Atonement for the High Priest

Aaron had to:

Kill the bullock and offer it as a sin offering for himself.

Take within the veil, alone, a censer of coals from the altar of incense.

Sprinkle the blood of the bullock once on the front of, and seven times before, the mercy seat, to make atonement for himself and for his household.

Atonement for the people

Aaron had to:

(Return to the outer court and) kill the goat for a sin offering for the people.

(return to the holy of holies and) sprinkle the blood of the goat once on the front of, and seven times before, the mercy seat, to make atonement for the holy place and for the tent of meeting, because of the sins of Israel.

(Return to the court and) sprinkle the blood of both the bullock and the goat seven times on the altar of sacrifice, to make atonement for it and to cleanse it.

Lay both hands on the head of the scapegoat.

Confess all the sins of the people and put them upon the head of the goat.

Send the goat into the wilderness, by the hand of an appointed man, to carry away the iniquities of the people of Israel.

Cleaning up

Aaron had to:

re-enter the holy place, bathe, and change his clothes

(Return to the outer court and) offer both rams as burnt offerings.

Burn the fat of the sin offerings upon the altar.

The man who led out the scapegoat to wash his clothes and bathe his body before returning to camp.

The remains of the sin offerings to be burned outside the camp.

The man who burnt them to wash his clothes, and bathe his body, before returning to camp.

EXPLANATORY NOTES ON LE 16.

- **"THE HOLY PLACE" (VS. 2).**

In this chapter, the *"holy of holies"* (Ex 36:33) is often referred to as the *"holy place"*, while the *"holy place"* is referred to as the *"tent of meeting"* (*"tabernacle of the congregation"* - A.V.) see verse 23. (Note, however, that vs. 24 probably refers to the outer court, where the laver was). The phrase, *"within the veil"* is also used for the *"holy of holies"*.

- **"LEST HE DIE" (VS. 1-2).**

Nadab and Abihu had both trespassed on God's holiness. The Day of Atonement now provided a clear pattern for entering the presence of God.

- **"BATHE HIS BODY" (VS. 4).**

Normally, only hands and feet were washed (Ex 40:30-33).

- **"PLAIN LINEN GARMENTS" (VS. 4).**

These garments were totally white, thus indicating purity (*"These are holy garments"*).

- **"SCAPEGOAT" (VS. 8).**

This term was first used by Tyndale, and has become part of everyday speech. However, the Hebrew reads literally, *"for Azazal"*. The meaning of this term is not clear, but the following suggestions have been made:

Azazel = *"sending away"* or *"entire removal"*, that is, removal of sins (*Beacon Comm., p. 365*).

Azazel = the name of a wilderness place where the goat was sent; perhaps a precipitous rock. The *Mishna* (Joma 6:6) suggests that the scapegoat was driven headlong over a cliff (Keil-Delitzsch, P. 404); this seems to have been done in the time of Christ, in any case (Jamieson, Fawcett & Brown, p. 97).

Azazel = Satan (e.g. deserts were seen as the abode of evil spirits - Is 13:21; 34:14; Mt 12:43; Re 18:2). The idea is that the goat takes Satan-inspired sins back to him again! (Keil-Delitzsch, p. 404).

In this concept, however, there is no suggestion whatever that the goat is offered to Azazel (Satan) as a sacrifice. "The sacrifice is made only to God". Nor is there any suggestion that the goat actually represents Satan - he does not; he represents only Christ.

Hence, both goats are referred to as a *single* offering (vs. 5).

The plain reason for using two goats is that one animal was insufficient to fulfil all the requirements of an adequate offering.

- **"SPRINKLING OF BLOOD" (VS. 14).**

The *"seven times"* seems to refer only to the sprinkling of the blood on the ground before the mercy seat (remember that *"seven"* is the number of perfection).

- **"EVERLASTING STATUTE" (VS. 34).**

The continuing need for atonement is thus stressed. So Jews today still observe *"yom kippur"* (= *"day of covering"*, that is, atonement), although, since they no longer have a divinely ordained altar or temple, without animal sacrifice.

It should be noted that the NT contains more exposition of the Day of Atonement than any other of Israel's observances. Large parts of the letter to the Hebrews are devoted to showing how the provisions of the Day of Atonement have been fulfilled in Christ, through his sacrificial death at Calvary, and through his resurrection and ascension.

- **THE FEAST OF BOOTHS** (Le 23:33-36, 39:43).

This feast lasted eight days, with the first and last days being *"holy convocations"*. The eighth day, however, was technically the climax, not just of this feast, but of all the feasts - for it was the last day of them all. There are more separate references to this feast than to any other of Israel's festivals.

For the first seven days, the feast was celebrated by the people dwelling in booths made of the branches of trees. Leviticus 23 specifically prescribes palm, willow and "leafy tree" branches.

In Ezra's day, olive, wild olive (pine?), and myrtle were also used (Ne 8:15) - that is, whatever was most suitable.

The whole feast was a time of rejoicing

> For the completion of the harvest (Le 23:39).

> For the protection of the Lord during their time in the wilderness (23:43).

This rejoicing was no doubt expressed in feasting, dancing and merriment (De 16:13-15; cp. Ne. 8:10-12; 1 Sa 30:16- the word *"feast"* comes from a Hebrew word denoting the circular motion of the dance).

This feast was remarkable for the extent of its offerings; the sacrifices at this time were more numerous than those required at any other time.

Daily sacrifices were offered as follows (Nu 29:12-38):

THE NORMAL DAILY OFFERINGS PLUS -

BURNT OFFERINGS
(Including cereal and drink offerings, as for the new moon).

SIN OFFERINGS

DAY	BULLOCKS	RAMS	LAMBS			GOATS
1	13	2	14	1	=	30
2	12	2	14	1	=	30
3	11	2	14	1	=	30
4	10	2	14	1	=	30
5	9	2	14	1	=	30
6	8	2	14	1	=	30
7	7	2	14	1	=	30
	70	14	98	7	=	189
8	1	1	1	1		

Note: that 7 bullocks were slain on the 7th day, and that the totals of all the sacrifices of the first seven days are multiples of seven.

- **HOW OFTEN WAS THE FEAST OF TABERNACLES CELEBRATED?**

It was, of course, an annual feast (2 Ch 8:13 etc.).

Since it was a commemoration of the protection of God during the wandering in the wilderness, it could not be kept until after Israel's arrival in Canaan.

The Temple

Biblical records of its celebration are . . .

In the days of Joshua (Ne 8:17).

In the days of Solomon (1 Kg 8:2, 65; 2 Ch 5:3; 7:8-20).

After the exile (Ez 3:4; Ne 8:14-18). This was the first time that booths had actually been constructed at the feast since Joshua's time (Ne 8:17).

In the days of Hosea (Ho 12:9).

In the days of Jesus (Jn 7:2 ff; note vs. 37-39).

By the time of Jesus, the celebration of the feast had been developed to include other features. For example, pharisaical instructions had been laid down, determining measurements and dimensions of the booths; and many other rules were also prescribed.

One of the more significant of these additions was a daily ceremony of drawing water. While the morning sacrifice was being prepared, a priest, accompanied by a procession of people, went to the Pool of Siloam and filled a golden pitcher with water. Others, meanwhile, were collecting willow branches from the Kidron valley. The great altar was canopied with the willow branches, and the water poured into a basin at the west of the altar. Wine was poured into a similar basin at the east. It is generally thought that this ceremony prompted the words of Jesus in Jn 7:37-39).

- **WHAT IS THE SIGNIFICANCE OF THE FEAST OF TABERNACLES FOR CHRISTIANS?**

(Before reading on, make a list of the typical significance you can personally see in the three parts of this feast.)

- **THE FEAST OF TRUMPETS**

New beginnings.

The seventh month of the Hebrew religious year was the first month of the civil year. The sounding of the *shophar* thus signifies new beginnings. Hearing the message of the gospel means a new start - a new life.

Preparation for atonement

By sounding at the beginning of the seventh month, the *shophar* proclaimed the coming of atonement (cp. the ministry of John the Baptist Mt 3:3 etc.).

Wherever and whenever the word of the Lord goes forth, warning of coming judgment on sin and proclaiming deliverance, the feast of trumpets is in a sense fulfilled (that is, the fulfilment cannot be restricted to just **one** event in history; it has many locations).

Warning of judgment

The trumpets will sound announcing the return of Christ and the judgments of God upon the earth. (Mt 24:31; 1 Th 4:16; cp. Jl 2:1, 15).

– THE DAY OF ATONEMENT

Similarities

This day clearly typifies the sacrifice of Christ at Calvary. Every detail is meaningful, but the following may be briefly noted:

Sacrifice - the first goat signifies Christ crucified (He 7:27).

Alone - only the high priest could make atonement; so Christ alone saves (He 9:7; 10:12).

Blood sprinkled seven times - signifies a perfect sacrifice (He 9:12-14).

Blood sprinkled before the mercy seat - indicates our righteous standing before God (Ro 5:1 ff).

Scapegoat - so Jesus carried our sins right away (He 9:26).

A day of complete rest - all of the people had to stand by and watch the high priest make atonement for them; no man could help the priest in his work; no man could assist in making atonement for himself. People are always trying to earn pardon by their own works, but it cannot be done. Only Christ could make sacrifice for us all, and now we are commanded to see in Christ alone our high priest, and to find in him alone eternal atonement (Ep 2:8-9; Jn 6:28-29; Tit 3:5).

Contrasts

There are also points of **contrast**. These are noted in Hebrews -

The cleansing of the high priest (our high priest is sinless already, 7:26-28).

The way into the holiest is now open to all (9:8; see also 4:14-16; 10:19-21). The high priest of Israel, by the strict ordinance of God, entered the holiest place on the Day of Atonement and on that day alone. Even then, death threatened him on entering, and he parted the veil with fear and trembling. By contrast, for us the veil has been utterly removed by Christ, and the way is made open to the presence of God.

Death threatens us if we fail to enter, and that daily!

Christ only needed to *"enter the holy of holies"* once for all (9:11-12).

His redemption is perfect and eternal (9:9, 12-14).

His covenant is a new covenant (9:15).

His *"tabernacle"* is heavenly (9:11, 24).

Christ only needed to offer himself once for all (9:25-28; 10:11-14).

Meditation:

Consider each of the above points and relate them to your own life.

Future

The day of atonement also speaks of the final, perfect cleansing of "Israel", that is, the people of God, descendants of Abraham (Ga 3:7,29); thus their redemption will be completed (Ro 3:19-24; 11:26-27). This will take place at the coming of Christ when our salvation as well as theirs will be fully revealed (1 Pe 1:5; 2 Th 1:10).

– THE FEAST OF BOOTHS

This feast signifies . . .

> The church's pilgrimage in this life, where we have *"no permanent dwelling"* (He 11:13-16); 2 Co 5:1-5).

Meditation:

What are the implications of this for our everyday life?

The protection of God upon us in this life (Ps 27:5; 91:1, 9; Is 4:5-6).

Our spiritual rest - in a sense, although pilgrims, we still enjoy the rest of faith (He 4:1 ff) in which we trust God for security and salvation.

Our heavenly rest - just as Israel celebrated the feast after their arrival in Canaan, so the church cannot find perfect rest until it inherits the Kingdom of God. Furthermore, the feast of booths was celebrated after the ingathering of the harvest - the harvest is the end of the age (Mt 13:39; Re 14:15). The harvest is both salvation and judgment (Mt 13:40; 2 Th 1:5ff), followed by the establishing of the Kingdom of

God (Mt 13:43). Then there will be another glorious celebration of the feast of booths. (Zc 14:16-19)!

Research:

Study these scriptures in relation to what you know about the Return of Christ.

The baptism in the Holy Spirit - see above, and Jn 7:37-39.

- Summary

The feasts of the seventh month have a twofold fulfilment -

Personal

The individual hears the sound of the word of God (Feast of Trumpets), accepts the salvation offered through the sacrifice of Jesus Christ (Day of Atonement), and enters a pilgrimage of faith, under the hand of God (feast of booths).

Prophetical

The trumpet sound will go forth (literally? metaphorically?) and announce the coming of Christ. At his coming, the church is finally cleansed (Day of Atonement) and the harvest completed. Then follows the rejoicing and relaxation of the Kingdom of God (feast of booths).

Read Isaiah chapter 12.

THE HEBREW YEAR

The Hebrew year was thus punctuated by three great feasts, each of which has a distinctive three-fold significance: historical, prophetical and personal.

Research: examine the chart of the feasts of Israel that is at the end of this book.

THE HISTORICAL SIGNIFICANCE OF THE THREE GREAT FEASTS

- Passover commemorated that incredible night when the Lord God "passed over" the houses of the Israelites and protected them from the angel of death. The covenant people of God were kept safe, and the next day a new nation was born. The former slaves cast aside their chains, and stepped into freedom and national independence.

- But freedom without a just law soon becomes licence, and licence debauchery. Pentecost therefore marked the giving of the law on Sinai, and the solemn acceptance of the covenant by the entire nation. Personal freedom was to be maintained under the law, and the law was seen as having its origin in God, as gaining its authority from him, and therefore as expressing eternal principles of upright social and religious behaviour.

- The nation now needed only a home. So the feast of tabernacles commemorated the establishment of Israel in the land of promise, their pleasant and peaceful home, after 40 years of living in tents while they wandered through the wilderness. They took boughs of palm, and willows of the brook, and out of them made temporary huts in which they lived during the feast. So in their fixed home and land of rest, their enjoyment was enhanced by the thankful and holy remembrance of past wanderings without a fixed dwelling. [24]

PERSONAL AND PROPHETICAL SIGNIFICANCE

- Passover points to the true Lamb of God, the Lord Jesus Christ. He is our Passover sacrifice, who was slaughtered for us that we might be purged of the corruption of sin, and might keep the feast with joy (1 Co 5:7-8).

- Pentecost points to the outpouring of the Holy Spirit, when the smoke and thunder of Sinai were replaced by the fiery tongues of the upper room, and when the law of death written on stones became the law of life engraved on human hearts. This living law seals God's covenant of grace with man more effectually than ever the old tablets could do.

- But having received redemption and the Spirit, we still lack a true home; we still look for the days of our wandering to cease. Tabernacles signifies the rest we find now in Christ, but even more the eternal home that awaits us in the city of God. Israel also, at the time of its future national regeneration (Ro 11:11-12), 25:32), will have cause to keep this feast again with immense joy.

- Added to this, in these three great feasts, there is a suggested picture of the Godhead: the Father as Creator, seen in the worship and joy of Tabernacles; the Son as Saviour, seen in the lamb of the Passover;

---

[24] Based on the article "Feasts", by A.R. Fausset, in his Bible Encyclopedia and Dictionary, Zondervan Publishing House, Grand Rapids, Michigan, no date given.

and the Holy Spirit as the new law-giver and the seal of God's covenant, portrayed in Pentecost.

RELATIONSHIP OF THE FEASTS

Is there a relationship between the feasts? That is, do all the feasts together represent some kind of divine timetable? In broad terms they do. So (as I have indicated above) in a **personal** sense

Passover	=	salvation
Pentecost	=	Holy Spirit baptism
Tabernacles	=	heavenly destiny

- And then in a ***prophetical*** sense -

Passover	=	Calvary
Pentecost	=	outpouring of the Spirit
Tabernacles	=	the return of Christ

As soon as details of these systems are examined, however, difficulties arise. Consider, for example, the following interpretation which has gained popularity in some parts of the church -

> Both Passover and Pentecost have been historical/ prophetical fulfilments; therefore, tabernacles must also have such a fulfilment. This is, in fact, taking place in our time.

> Right now the trumpets are sounding, calling all true Christians together (Nu 10:1 ff.) and to be *"overcomers"* (Jl. 2; Re 1-3). Only those who are obedient to the call of God, who *"hear the trumpets"*, will be able to *"appropriate"* the benefits of *"the day of atonement"* which must quickly follow.

> This prophetic *"day of atonement"* is still future, and when it comes the obedient church will (for the first time ever) "appropriate the absolute fullness of the

cross of Christ". At this point the true church (those who have *"heard the trumpets"*) will be cleansed from every spot and blemish (Ep 5:25 ff; Ro 8:16-23). That true and overcoming church will then have been brought into a state of "perfection".

On that day there will be a "visible, literal, and spiritual manifestation of the Lord Jesus Christ" to the purified church (He 9:28).

The "harvest" will then be completed in the intervening "four days" (Le 23:39; De 16:13; Mt 13:39); then will follow 3 1/2 years of the Great Tribulation, during which the perfected church, the spotless Bride of Christ, will be caught away *"into the wilderness"* (Re 12:1 ff.) to rejoice in *"the feast of tabernacles"*.

That will be followed, *"on the eighth day"*, by the return of Christ, the resurrection of the dead, and the millennium.

COMMENTS

There are weaknesses in the teaching outlined above -

- ### BASIC SUPPOSITIONS

    First of all, it assumes that because Tabernacles came after Passover and Pentecost, all typological and spiritual aspects of Tabernacles must also come after those 2 feasts - including atonement. Hence, a new interpretation of atonement is essential, although it flies in the face of the teaching of the book of Hebrews! (Thus, a basic rule of hermeneutics is broken).

    The answer is not to change one's interpretation of Hebrews, but to look at one's pre-suppositions. Consider the following (and see chart just below):

If it be accepted that Tabernacles must have an historical/prophetical fulfilment, the question is, when?

For example, if Pentecost was fulfilled literally 50 days after Passover (Calvary), then Tabernacles should have been fulfilled 4 months later! (That is, AD 30).

If it be suggested that Pentecost was not fulfilled till the 20th century, then Tabernacles is not due for another 5000 or so years! (One suggestion to counteract this is that the 2000 paces of Joshua 3:4 signify 2000 years from Passover to Tabernacles! If that's true, anything can mean anything!) Either way, we cannot have Tabernacles beginning to be fulfilled now.

The simplest view is that all of the feasts have a relevance to every age. (For example, when have the trumpets **not** been sounding? When has atonement **not** been possible?)

• MEANING OF WORDS

Which is the "church" spoken of in Ep 5:22 ff? Is it not the one for which Christ died? The church for all time? How can it possibility be taken to mean only the church alive before Christ's coming? If it is, the rest of the church is damned -for Christ neither loved it, nor died for it. (See also Ro 8:17 ff. The word "us" shows that Paul expected to be in it!) Further, it is assumed that the trumpets used at the Feast of Trumpets were silver trumpets, as in Nu 10. This is, of course, not so.

	14	Passover
First Month	15	
	21	Unleavened Bread
Second Month		
Third Month	6	Pentecost
Fourth Month		
Fifth Month		
Sixth Month		
Seventh Month	1	Trumpets
	10	Atonement
	15	
	22	Booths

- **THE RETURN OF CHRIST**

How can Christ return twice? He 9:28 does not teach a return day only for believers. It is a return for all - but it will bring salvation to believers only.

- **THE WILDERNESS**

The idea of the Bride being "caught away into the wilderness" is based on a special (and rather suspect) interpretation of Re 12. This is an admittedly difficult chapter, and there is a legion of possible interpretations. It violates one of the basic rules of hermeneutics to build a major doctrine on a passage of scripture which abounds in esoteric prophetic symbolism. The fact is, outside of a singular interpretation of Re 12, there is no other evidence of the scheme presented in the above description.

- **OTHER COMMENTS**

It is unrealistic to assume that every detail of the feasts (or of any aspect of Israel's ancient ceremonies) can be fitted into a rigid prophetic scheme. And the attempt to do so often leads to some absurd conclusions.

For example, what do you make of the following claims? They come from the same source as the above description: that every detail of the feasts can be fitted into a rigid prophetic scheme. So the same teaching claims

that 5 priests blew the trumpets (=5 ministry gifts), although two were already dead (Nu 3:1-5)

that the united sound of the trumpets was a miracle (2 Ch 5:1-13), whereas it was simply harmony

That it is the **Bride's** duty to bring in the poor and the lame, (Mt 22:1-14 etc.)

That the woman of Re 12 is carried away by an eagle; and so on!

- **DANGEROUS IMPLICATIONS**

Considerable attention has been given to these views because of their dangerous implications. They claim to be the answer to the so-called lack of spirituality in churches today - even amongst charismatics. They appeal to the unwary by a promise of easy spirituality - ("one day you will be perfect with no effort at all".) They keep attention on the future. And they are divisive, suggesting an exclusive body (the Bride) which is different from the rest of the church. These views seem very spiritual (everyone wants to be perfect - to see the church in its glory) but they actually take people away from the basic principles of Christian victory through identification with Christ.

You should beware of interpretations of biblical types which pay too much attention to particular details. They will generally lead to foolish and speculative ideas.

The same may also be said of the parables of Jesus. Attempts to give a spiritual meaning to every detail of the parables have led to preposterous conclusions, and sometimes plain heresy. The parables are best interpreted broadly, as Jesus himself did; and so are the types. [25]

---

[25] Notice the single lesson Jesus drew from each of these parables: Mt 18:23-35; 20:1-16; 25:1-13; 25:14-30; etc. In these other parables, Jesus offered a more detailed application of the stories, but still left many details unexplained, because they were simply to bring colour

You would find it a very useful lesson in hermeneutics to look up in your NT all of the parables of Jesus, and all of the references to OT types. The manner in which Jesus interpreted the parables, and in which both he and the apostles applied the types, should provide a defence for you against many of the wild and unsubstantiated ideas which are so often presented to unwary Bible students.

Closing Meditation: Read 1 Kg 12:32-33; 13:1-34 in the light of 1 Co 5:8.

(A chart of the feasts and their associated sacrifices is printed on the next page.)

---

and cohesion to the stories: Mt 13:3-23; 13:24-29; 13:36-42; 22:1-14; etc.

	Name of Feast	Date of Cele-bration	Central Feature	Historical Signifi-cance	Prophetical Signifi-cance	Typical Significance
(A) March / April *First Fruits*	Pass-over (Ex 12:1-28)	14th day of 1st month	Slaying and eating of lamb	a) Deliver-ance from Egypt b) Sacred New Year	a) Death of Jesus b) New Gospel Age	a) Deliverance from sin b) New Life
	Un-leavened Bread (Le 23:6-14)	15th to 21st days of 1st month	Eating of un-leavened bread	a) Sorrow for past suffer-ing b) Freedom from corruption of Egypt	a) Sufferings of Christ b) Sinless-ness of Christ	a) Repentance b) Holy Life
(B) May/June *Harvest*	Pente-cost (Le 23:15-21)	6th day of 3rd month	Offering of two leavened loaves	a) Giving of law at Sinai b) Fruitless-ness	Outpouring of Spirit at Jerusalem	a) Baptism in Spirit b) Fruit and gifts of Spirit
(C) September / October *Ingathering*	Trum-pets (Le 23:23-25)	1st day of 7th month	Blowing of **Shophar**	a) Civil New Year b) Announc-ing of sacred month	b) Announc-ing of Christ's coming	a) Repentance b) Readiness for Christ's coming
	Atone-ment (Le 23:26-32; Le 16:3-10)	10th day of 7th month	Sin offerings bulls and goats; blood sprinkled in holy of holies	Shedding and applying of blood for remission of sins	a) Death of Jesus b) Final cleansing of Israel	Remission of sins through faith in shed blood of Christ
	Taber-nacles (Le 23:33-36, Le 23:39-43)	15th to 22nd days of 7th month	Dwelling in booths	a) The Lord's protection during pilgrimage b) Rest from wandering in wilder-ness	Kingdom of God on earth	a) Pilgrimage and rest in Christ b) Future heavenly home

BIBLIOGRAPHY

Chant, Barry, *The Secret Is Out*. Luke Publications.

Chant, Ken, *Understanding Your Bible*. Vision Publishing.

Fausett, A. R., *Bible Encyclopedia and Dictionary*. Zondervan Publishing House: Grand Rapids, Michigan.

Josephus, *Antiquities*.

Keil and Delitzsch, *Commentary on the Old Testament*. Eerdmans Pub. Co., Grand Rapids, Michigan, 1976.

Merrill C. Tenney, editor. *Pictorial Encyclopedia of the Bible*. Zondervan Publishing House: Michigan, 1975.

Slemming, Charles, *Made According To Pattern*. Christian Literature Crusade: Fort Washington, Pennsylvania, 1974.

_____. Charles, *These Are The Garments*. Christian Literature Crusade: Fort Washington, Pennsylvania, 1974.

_____. Charles, *Thus Shalt Thou Serve*. Christian Literature Crusade: Fort Washington, Pennsylvania, 1974.

Unger, M. *Bible Dictionary*. Moody Press: 1957.

Wemp, C. Sumner, *Teaching From the Tabernacle*. Moody Press: Chicago, 1976

Lightning Source UK Ltd.
Milton Keynes UK
UKHW021841090223
416682UK00012B/705

9 781615 290918